A HACKNEY
CENTURY
1900–1999

The Old Church Tower of St John at Hackney under repair. Scheduled as an ancient monument, the tower was acquired by Hackney Council under the Hackney Borough Council Act of 1932. Repairs are in progress by church builders Dove Brothers in this view of about 1933.

A HACKNEY
CENTURY
1900–1999

❧ D A V I D   M A N D E R ❧

LONDON BOROUGH OF HACKNEY
SUTTON PUBLISHING

British Library Cataloguing in Publication Data
A catalogue record for this book is available from
the British Library.

ISBN 0-7509-2033-2

ALAN SUTTON™ and SUTTON™ are the trade
marks of Sutton Publishing Limited

Typeset in 11/14pt Photina.
Typesetting and origination by
Sutton Publishing Limited.
Printed in Great Britain by
Redwood Books, Trowbridge, Wiltshire.

Front cover: A range of folk from Hackney's busy twentieth century. Among views not included elsewhere in the book are: the Reader family in the garden of 28 Christie Road with engines, 1909 (top right); VE-day party in Essex Street, Hoxton, 1945 (top centre) and a selection of Hackney children, 1994 (bottom centre). Thanks to Geoff Wilson (children, bottom centre), David Hoffman (council workers, bottom right), Michael Kirkland (Rushmore School, bottom left and Hackney Old Church Tower) and Chris Dorley-Brown (tower block). Design work by David Mander and Michael Kirkland. Montage work by Michael Kirkland. *Half-title page*: Mobile sports in action, 1984. Photograph, David Hoffman. *Title page*: A summer afternoon outing to Clissold Park, *c.* 1910, with the bandstand and the spire of St Mary's new church in the background.

Acknowledgements

The author would like to thank all those who allowed their photographs or copies of them to be used in this book, in particular Mrs Josephine Boyle (pp. 22 top and middle, 29 middle), Mr G.A. Butters (p. 22 bottom), Mrs G. Fillery (p. 69 bottom), *The Hackney Gazette* (p. 42 bottom), D. Jones (p. 60 bottom), Mr Newton (pp. 15 bottom, 29 top), The Pedro Club (p. 98 middle), Mrs Rapson (p. 47 top), Royal Commission for Historic Manuscripts (p. 95 bottom left), Mr Don Ruston (p. 34 top), Mr Dick Whetstone (pp. 14 top and bottom, 25 bottom left and right, 40 middle), Mrs E. Whitby (p. 68 bottom).

Individual photographers are credited against their photographs. Special thanks to Chris Dorley-Brown, Pam Isherwood, Geoff Wilson, Paul Stewart, Val Wilmer and Chris Wood. Every effort was made to contact photographers to obtain permission to use their material; the publisher and author regret that it was not possible to contact all those whose material appears in this book.

Thanks are also due to Michael Kirkland, Martin Taylor and Karyn Stavert of Hackney Archives Department, who helped in the production of the book.

Wick girls just want to have fun. A party from Gainsborough Road School at Ramsgate in the 1920s.

Contents

St Leonard's Church, Shoreditch, seen from the North
London Railway bridge about 1900. George Dance's
church was to survive two world wars, but at the
century's close still needs extensive repair work.

Out with the old, in with the new. Proclamation of Edward VII on the steps of Hackney's second town hall, January 1901.

Introduction

Welcome to the souvenir of the century – for those who lived through it and those who wish to know more about Hackney's very varied twentieth century. What follows is a sampler from the growing visual collections held by Hackney Council's Archives Department, and marks the tenth year that Hackney Archives Department and Sutton Publishing have worked together to publish books on the pictures and history of Hackney.

A Hackney Century is intended to take the reader through time on a visual journey through Hackney, Shoreditch and Stoke Newington, with each chapter providing snapshots of the decade. This is not a history, nor can it be comprehensive, since there are many aspects of life in Hackney that are under-represented in the visual collections held at Hackney Archives Department. Some of these omissions are a mark of what was not recorded photographically at different times. Internal views of houses of all classes are uncommon, though we are lucky in having the views of the upper-middle-class Gaviller house at Lower Clapton from 1910, the slum views of the 1930s, and the interior of a postwar council flat. Not all themes are covered with equal strength in each decade – there has been more political material as the twentieth century draws to its close. This was not because Hackney was any less a political place in earlier decades, merely that the material has not come into Hackney's archives, or survived in places where it can be reproduced within the budget available from the publisher. A case in point is the struggle over Hackney Council's intention to clear the vast majority of private housing in the 1960s and replace it with council estates. It took a major battle for protestors to preserve De Beauvoir Town north of Downham Road, overturning a scheme which would have kept De Beauvoir Square – but not the houses round it. The result was a significant victory for those who wished to reverse the wholesale destruction of the Georgian- and Victorian-built environment, but without the photographs, it cannot feature in the body of this book.

However, a number of themes run through *A Hackney Century*. Each chapter has some street views recording physical change and buildings that have vanished as the century has progressed. There is strong coverage of shops and markets, schools, transport, religion, and Hackney's waterways. The later chapters include material on some of Hackney's ethnic minority communities. Until recently the archive collection at Hackney was weak on such material; the addition of more recent records transferred from the Press and Public Relations section of Hackney Council, and the deposit of the photographic files of one of Hackney's radical papers, the *Hackney People's Press* have helped fill some of the gaps. An appeal via the *Hackney Gazette* also prompted one photographer to come forward and this helped strengthen the last two chapters, which include positive images as well as those that cover the results of racism and policing issues.

In previous books I have indicated that gaps in the photographic record exist because photographs were not taken. I was reminded of this during the compilation of this book. I had hoped to include a photograph of the Nation of Islam in action outside the Kingsland Shopping Centre, but had to desist in taking a view of my own in the face of direct threats from members of that church. In other cases the views do exist, but could not have been used in a work of local history without paying substantial reproduction fees. I am very grateful to those contemporary local photographers who have allowed their work to be reproduced. Under current copyright legislation it will be at least another hundred years before a book of this nature can appear which will be able to make better use of what is now contemporary material.

My first selection of views from Hackney's collections, *The London Borough of Hackney in Old Photographs before 1914*, and the second, produced with Jenny Golden, *The London Borough of Hackney in Old Photographs 1890–1960*, are now both out of print. The first book was published in 1989 and since then the reprographic quality of the publisher's work has improved considerably. Consequently, I have taken the opportunity of including a number of views from both earlier books on the basis that they deserve a second showing in a better guise.

The advances in digital image storage and manipulation have already made a dramatic impact on the way we are able to view, store and reproduce historic pictures. Although this book has been reproduced by conventional means, the technology and skills available to the staff of Hackney Archives Department have played their part in the creation of the book. I wanted the cover to convey the strength and diversity of the communities that have made up Hackney over the last hundred years, and the montage on the cover is intended to reflect this. Selection of images for large parts of the book was greatly speeded up by the use of Hackney Archives Department's *Hackney on Disk* map and image system. This system, which links pictures to maps, enabling the user to draw a box on the map to retrieve and display pictures on a computer screen, also has a number of conventional search mechanisms, including one that allows the collection of digital images (now numbering about 11,000) to be searched by date. Some images whose quality was not good enough to be reproduced in previous books have also been copied digitally for this book. The firewood seller on p. 46 was copied from a contemporary local Liberal Party newspaper; balances in contrast were changed in the picture to hold the contrast on the firewood seller's face while bringing the prospective Parliamentary candidate out of the shadows. Similarly, the wedding at Mare Street Baptist Church on p. 22 has also been treated. The Butters family took two photographs, one that showed the arriving wedding guests but not the top part of the church, and the other that included the whole church but only some of the guests. The roof and top details of the church from the latter have been digitally added to the former giving a complete picture. However, no digital manipulation of any image has taken place to alter content within the frame. What there was is what is reproduced on the page.

Future developments are already planned and will include access to some of our photographic collection via our web site (http://www.hackney.gov.uk). Hackney Archives Department has worked in partnership with the National Trust's Sutton House, who have produced an educational programme for children on Victorian Hackney, and plans are in hand to explore Tudor Hackney through a similar programme using a virtual reality recreation of a long lost house. It may be possible to produce CD ROM selections of our picture collections in future to supplement conventional photographic books. If you are interested in these possibilities, then please contact us. The address to write or e-mail to is in the penultimate paragraph of this introduction.

The pictures that make up *A Hackney Century* owe much to those who have given or deposited photographs and records of Hackney people and organisations to Hackney Archives Department. If the record of daily life in contemporary Hackney is to be as strong as the record of the past, then the help of local people, and those who have past associations with the area, will continue to be needed. Original items can be loaned for copying, and if the original has been damaged or creased, then we may be able to produce a digital copy that will remove some or even all of the damage.

Although considerable research has gone into the writing of the captions, there may be others whose local knowledge exceeds my own, or who can fill in gaps in the text. If you can help then please write to me at Hackney Archives Department, 43 De Beauvoir Road, London N1 5SQ, or e-mail on archives@hackney.gov.uk. We can also supply digital copies of most of the photographs and other prints in this book either from our own printers or photographically. A price list is available from us – please include an A5-sized sae. For copyright material, we can put customers in contact with the relevant photographer. For those who would like to be kept in regular touch with the work and collections of Hackney Archives Department, and receive news of forthcoming publications, the Friends of Hackney Archives provides four newsletters a year and an annual magazine, *Hackney History*. Subscriptions start at £8.00 p.a. for individual membership. Details are available via Hackney Archives Department.

I hope you enjoy your commemorative souvenir of what has been a busy and active century for Hackney. At the time of writing the council is undergoing financial problems; in the course of researching this book I was amused to find references to Hackney Borough Council's difficulties in balancing the books at the turn of the century. It is only to be hoped that the coming century is a more secure and prosperous one for both the council and the communities who make Hackney an exciting place to live and work.

David Mander, July 1999

The Edwardians:
1900–1910

The offices of the *Hackney Gazette* at 440 Kingsland Road at the junction of
Richmond Road, about 1905. Founded in 1864, the *Gazette* was soon taken over by
Charles Potter, and printed from Lenthall works a little further east on Richmond
Road. The *Gazette* moved from these offices in 1924 and is now published from
offices in Bethnal Green.

The bustle of South Hackney Broadway (now part of Lauriston Road), with a horse tram heading for the terminus at the west end of Cassland Road. Photograph, Charles Martin, 1904.

Women cross the Cat and Mutton bridge over the Regent's Canal to shop in the Broadway, London Fields, 1905.

Each of the gates to Victoria Park had its attendant public house. This is the Royal Hotel on Lauriston Road. A urinal stands prominently outside and a stallholder awaits custom by the gate – possibly selling ice creams; this was to be a popular patch for ice-cream sellers over the ensuing ninety years.

The Red Lion, Church Street, Stoke Newington and a glimpse up the narrow end of Lordship Lane (now Red Lion Lane), about 1900. Rebuilt in 1924, the pub is now the Magpie and Stump.

Ten years before this Alfred Braddock view of about 1900 was taken, Sutton House had been reunited as the St John's Church Institute. Built in 1535 for Sir Ralph Sadleir, it was divided into two houses in about 1751, known by the end of the nineteenth century as Milford and Picton Houses. Acquired by the National Trust in 1938, today it is an active community resource and is Hackney's oldest surviving house.

Upper Clapton Road and the junction with Lea Bridge Road in 1907. The horse is very much in evidence, pulling carts, the horse bus and the horse tram on the left. The motor bus is a sign of changing times, but the horse trams had another two years of service before electricification. Photograph, Alfred Braddock.

Goulton Road from Lower Clapton Road in 1906. Photographer Alfred Braddock seemed to have a magic ability to conjure policemen out of the blue as soon as he set up his camera, willing to pose in all weathers. For many years the shops on the corner, which probably dated back to the eighteenth century, were kept by George Pratt, tailor and Charles Witherden, butcher. Bomb damage in 1940 resulted in demolition after the war.

Governing Stoke Newington was guaranteed to build up an appetite. This was the scene just before coffee at a dinner given in honour of Thomas Coram in 1900. The bearded clergyman presiding was Prebendary Shelford, chairman of the vestry. After an uneasy period of governance by the Hackney Board of Works, Stoke Newington regained its independence in 1894 and was to become a metropolitan borough later in 1900.

Broad Street station was built in 1865 for the North London Railway to enable them to take commuters directly into the City. Although the frontage lay in the City, much of the eastern side of the station lay in Shoreditch. Construction cut through parts of the site of the medieval priory of Holy Trinity. The line was closed in 1985 and the station demolished in the following year. Broadgate now occupies the site and the boundaries were altered in 1990 so that the whole area now comes within the City of London.

Motor buses began to be a common sight on Hackney roads from 1905 onwards. Competition between rival operators was fierce and when in 1912 the London and General Omnibus group became part of the Underground railway group, rival Metropolitan Electric Tramways planned to introduce a new fleet of Daimler buses. This example, in a royal blue livery on Route 57 to Stoke Newington, was probably photographed not long after the new service began in January 1913. However, by then the rival companies had merged, and the fleet was one of those that passed to London Transport in 1933.

Our turn of the century shopping expedition starts with E. Stepney's tobacconist and newsagent at 456 Kingsland Road in 1907. With bomb outrages, troubles with railway companies and a campaign under way for the Unionists in Northern Ireland, the news stories could be as applicable at both ends of the century.

Henry Krantz's music store at No. 3 Lea Bridge Road (renumbered 5 in 1903). In an era that preceded television and radio, the piano was common in many homes, and tuning, repair work and selling sheet music could support a business.

F.J. Esdaile's draper and millinery shop, 10 Clarence Road, about 1905. The rolls of cloth are a reminder that women made some of their own clothing at home. Hackney had its own department stores, but corner shops could successfully compete for local trade.

Most of Hackney's heavy industry was concentrated in the Wick, but Lewis Berger & Sons' paint factory had occupied this site north of Morning Lane since 1780. The warehouse on the left was built over the course of the Hackney Brook and lay just beyond the site of the laboratory block of 1934, which still stands, in use as council offices. The road on the right is the eastern end of Hockley Street, cleared in the 1930s.

Repairs are under way to the culvert that carried the Hackney Brook under Mare Street, about 1900. A policeman stands in front of a steam lorry in the background. Culverting of Hackney Brook had been completed in 1859–60, achieving its transformation from a comparatively clean stream to part of London's sewage system. Today only the dip under the railway bridge marks what was once a ford, but when the surrounding brickwork has failed during times of heavy rain the water still has the power to burst to the surface, though it is over thirty years since the last flood.

Hackney built its own electricity generating plant in 1901 and began a programme to replace gas street lights, introduced in 1856–7, which needed lighting each evening. Lamplighters and other colleagues who made up the Hackney muster of the Gas Light and Coke Company posed for their photograph at the east end of Paragon Road in October 1906. Main roads were arc-lit before the First World War, but the majority of Hackney's back streets still had no cabling well into the 1920s.

Hackney Union Workhouse was built on the old parish workhouse site on Homerton High Street between 1838 and 1842 and provided accommodation for both the able bodied and the infirm. This view of a nurse and an omnibus pram was taken in the grounds in 1902.

Left: Sedan chair transport for one of the aged, 1902. *Right*: The union workhouses had been intended to remove the majority of payments to non-resident paupers, but some 'relief' was still paid. This is the female waiting room in 1902. The workhouses closed in 1930. Hackney's became a hospital, used latterly for old people, when its reputation was almost as bad as in workhouse days.

Above: Strong's Farm stood on the west bank of the Hackney Cut. Properly it was 'Lock House', built by the River Lee Trustees, who had constructed the Cut in the 1770s. The lock, to the south of the bridge, was removed about 1865. The alternative name came from James Strong, dairyman, who lived here from the early 1880s until 1911. The bridge was replaced by a weir further south along the channel between 1930 and 1936 and Weir Cottage now stands on the site of Lock House, which was demolished in 1912. This photograph dates from *c.* 1900.

Right: Dog days on one of the East London Water Works reservoirs in Walthamstow for one of the Hanbury family from Stainforth House about 1900. The first three of these were built in 1863, followed by a further two three years later and a further three in 1867–8.

Cavalry and bunting greeted the Prince and Princess of Wales who came to open the new Central Library on Mare Street on 28 May 1908. Attempts to provide Hackney with a free library service had been defeated in the nineteenth century, though both Shoreditch and Stoke Newington had public libraries by the turn of the century.

The King's Hall and Baths, Lower Clapton Road and the crowd appears to have stopped for Alfred Braddock and his box camera. The baths, designed by Harnor and Pinches, were opened in 1897. One of the baths was designed to have a planked stage laid over it to provide a hall for lectures and entertainments.

An outing from school on Empire Day in Clissold Park, May 1902. This celebration of Britain's imperial domain was a feature of school life into the 1930s.

For Empire Day in 1909 the children of Berger Road take a sash and in some cases a bit of costume for a tableau. Britannia presides triumphant in the middle.

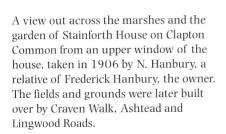

A view out across the marshes and the garden of Stainforth House on Clapton Common from an upper window of the house, taken in 1906 by N. Hanbury, a relative of Frederick Hanbury, the owner. The fields and grounds were later built over by Craven Walk, Ashtead and Lingwood Roads.

The front of Springfield House, about 1900. The house and its grounds were incorporated into the newly formed Springfield Park in 1905. The family group, with mother and father seated and children by the trees suggests that this view belongs to the last period of private occupancy, when the occupier was Frank Collins, a builder.

The power of the school caretaker is well demonstrated in this view of 'Mr Newman's china garden' in the grounds of Homerton Board School, Chatham Place and seen here in 1904. Newman constructed his garden from bits of crockery and bones, including horse and hyenas – you can always find the odd bit of hyena bone in Hackney when you need it. In the aftermath of the Boer War Newman made a statue out of the Afrikaan leader Kruger 'from the bones of a defunct house'. The garden proved a popular place with courting couples – there really is no accounting for taste. . . .

The Boer War saw a spate of patriotic melodrama, and Shoreditch's Britannia Theatre, looking for new directions in the aftermath of the death of its ruling matriarch and wife of the founder, Sara Lane, in 1899, was happy to give it a try. *Soldiers of the Queen* featured in the 1902 season. Sadly in a era of changing taste the 'Brit' could not hold on to its audiences and after several changes of management, the Britannia became a cinema in 1923, finally closing its doors after bombing in 1940.

Tom and Annie Reader, with children Annie Cecilia and baby Marie, with her nurse and members of the Wenzel family, gathered in the back garden of 21 Groombridge Road in 1901. The Wenzels were near neighbours from 275 Victoria Park Road.

'And this one was forty, love' . . . Summer afternoon tennis has paused for a moment in Victoria Park, c. 1908.

Carriages unload yet more guests at a Butters family wedding at Mare Street Baptist Church, around 1900. Founded at the end of the eighteenth century, the congregation continued to have a strong middle-class element to it in the years up to the First World War. This building of 1855 was damaged in 1940 and left an empty shell by a V2 in 1945. The congregation re-formed, but on a new site, and now worship at Frampton Park Baptist

From Peace to War:
1910–1919

Sion House, No. 187 Lower Clapton Road, opposite the pond, was up for rent in 1911. Built for James Limborough in 1768, the house was one of a number of grand merchant houses that had survived into a changing era. Formerly home to the Berger family (paint makers), it had just been vacated by Dr Christopher Maitland. The house had eleven bedrooms, drawing, dining, and morning rooms, three parlours, stables for three horses and three-quarters of an acre of garden. Sion House remained empty until about 1918, when it was taken by the Hackney Volunteer Social Club. Despite local protests it was included in the compulsory purchase made by Hackney Council for the first Powell House estate and demolished in March 1933.

An electric tram is about to pass under Mare Street's North London Railway bridge – and what better place to advertise beer? In this view of about 1915 the Hackney Furnishing Company occupy the former draper's shop of Green and Branscombe, a building whose façade hides an early eighteenth-century structure visible in the earliest surviving drawings of this part of what was once Hackney's Church Street. A substantial oak staircase which may have dated from the seventeenth century still survived in the house in the mid-1890s. On the left are the range of shops built after the road widening approved in 1899 and completed in 1906.

Hoxton Street, looking north from the Queens Head public house with the workhouse relieving office in the background, about 1905. John James Sainsbury took over a cheese shop from his brother-in-law Edward Staples at No. 183 about 1883. By 1901 the branch had moved over the road to Nos 180–2, but closed around 1916.

Relatively empty roads make it easy to cross and shop at the west end of Graham Road around 1910. The tram has paused just to the west of the track loop before the single line swing round into the top end of Mare Street. The shop on the left was Smart and Smart's home furnishing emporium.

Broadway Market from London Fields, with the Cat and Mutton public house on the left. Named simply 'The Broadway' until 1937, the first row of shops here was built as Duncan Place at the north end in the late 1820s. In Edwardian times it was one of Hackney's many busy local shopping streets.

Left: When horses still played an important part in transporting people and goods, livings could be made from a range of associated trades. This is Frank Fordham's harness shop at 28 Dalston Lane, about 1910. The business moved from Lee Street in 1906 to No. 22 and to No. 28 the following year. It had closed by 1914. *Right*: A.H. Sexton, son and dog stand outside the family newsagents, 56 Cadogan Terrace, about 1914.

Milk to the door. Employees of T. Brassington's Royal College Dairy, including A.G. Jones on the left, stand with three barrows, probably not far away from No. 253 Amhurst Road, where the business was based. It was run by Isabella Brassington from 1900 to 1911.

Dignitaries, including Hackney's Mayor and Mayoress Cllr and Mrs Henry Davenport, stand outside the newly opened Homerton Library on Brooksby's Walk on 17 May 1913. Designed by Edwin Cooper, the branch closed in 1974, superseded by the present library on Homerton High Street. Shortly afterwards it became the Chats Palace arts and community centre.

Kingsland Road, looking north, with the fire station of 1895 and, in the distance, the Metropolitan Hospital of 1886. The present fire station on the same site was completed in 1977.

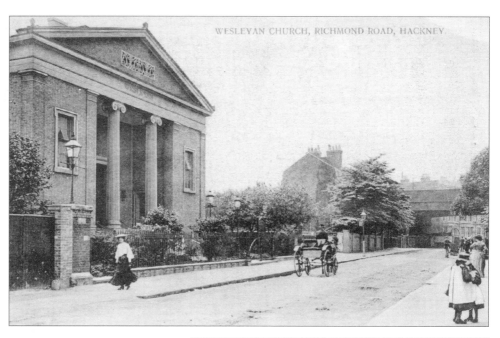

A page of churches begins with Richmond Road Wesleyan Chapel, which stood on the south side of that road, east of the junction with what is now Martello Street. Built in 1846, and with a Sunday school on its west side, the chapel closed in 1925, when the Methodist Central Hall on Mare Street opened. Leased to the Central Hackney Synagogue, an Orthodox congregation, it remained a place of worship until 1958.

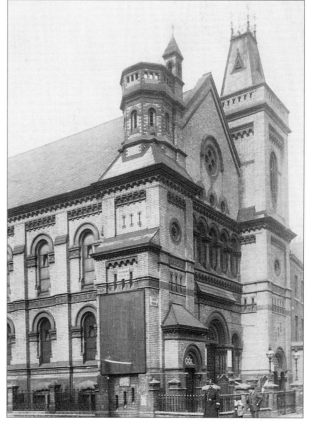

Left: St Mary's new church, Stoke Newington, was having the floor renewed when this view of the nave was taken in 1917. Designed by Sir George Gilbert Scott, the church was completed in 1858. *Right*: The United Methodist Church on the corner of East Road and Fairbank Street, about 1910. Built in the early 1870s as the Jubilee Chapel of the 'Bible Christians' and becoming Methodist in the 1890s, the chapel ceased to be a place of worship in 1952. By the following year it was the Jubilee Studio of the BBC and was a theatre organ studio. The BBC left in 1965 and it had been demolished by 1968.

Workhouses also had a medical role. Here staff of Hackney Workhouse infirmary pose by a Model T Ford motor ambulance outside the workhouse, about 1919.

Left: The west frontage of Shoreditch Workhouse on Hoxton Street included the Guardian's relieving offices, built in 1863. Originally the site of the workhouse had been a parochial estate known as the Land of Promise and this singularly inappropriate name for a union workhouse was retained for the narrow lane that lay to the south of the offices. Today only the façade of the relieving offices remains, incorporated into new housing association offices and the dead-end lane has lost its name. Time to revive the Land of Promise? *Right*: Disaster struck for Mrs Dunsdon of Gifford Street, Hoxton in July 1911, when her husband was killed (presumably in a fall) when hanging up decorations outside their house for the local celebrations of the Coronation of 1911. The *Daily Graphic* took up her cause and in September she received a charitable payment from the new King. The 46-year-old widow had to support five children on odd washing jobs and with the small earnings of her two eldest. Besides publicity, the newspaper also offered assistance from its relief fund.

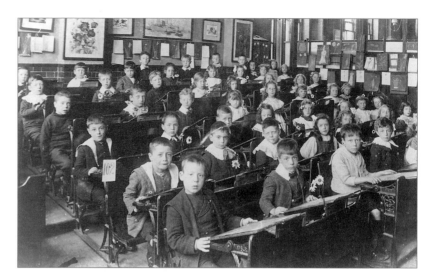

A pause in the drawing lesson for a junior class at Gayhurst Road School in 1910.

Charles Layzell and the South Hackney Central School orchestra, about 1919. Opened as Cassland Road Higher School in 1902, the mixed Central School had taken over from a girls' secondary school by 1919. Merged with Lauriston School in 1951, the school was one of those that formed Kingsland School in 1982.

'Exercise for workmen's sons: boys being taught boxing at Pitfield Street Baths' was the caption for this photograph that appeared in *Black and White* on 4 February 1911. Shoreditch Borough Council had just decided to open the baths (which stood to the south of the former Shoreditch Library) as a gymnasium. Although some members of the council were opposed to the move, boxing was widely regarded as essential healthy exercise for working-class boys and cost 2*d* (0.83p) a night.

The quiet of a respectable middle-class street. This was part of the east side of Culford Road near the junction with the present Northchurch Road. J. Seeley's building business occupies the corner premises. Culford Road had been laid out by 1843, but these houses here date from about 1848. Photograph *c.* 1912.

The Hope public house stood on the west side of the part of Holly Street that lies to the north of Forest Road and is seen here about 1912. This part of the road, built in the 1830s, was cleared in the 1960s but the Hope lasted until 1975. Skelton Close now occupies the site.

Another quiet street whose appearance was to be transformed in the second half of the century was Handley Road, which originally ran north from Victoria Park Road to King Edward's Road. This view of about 1910 was taken at the northern end – the junction with Southborough Road is on the left where the road bends. The majority of houses still have their cast-iron railings, lost in the scrap drives of the Second World War. Worse was to befall this part of the road, which was all cleared in the late 1960s for the architecturally brutal Kingshold estate. It was not until the late 1990s that parts of this estate were demolished and the old road pattern restored.

North-eastern Hackney was the last part of the parish to retain the appearance of countryside. This is Spring Hill in 1912, seen from the path along the River Lea, with Spring Hill Farm on the left. In 1774 this had been part of the estate of Thomas Webbe, with a tile yard and wharves on a creek called Giles Dock that ran immediately behind Spring Hill Farm. Giles Dock had been filled in by 1894, but with the creation of Springfield Park in 1905, the farm and the buildings beyond were earmarked for removal. This view was taken as a record prior to demolition.

The view down Little Hill, about 1910. This narrow alley ran from Mount Pleasant Lane down to the Lea just south of the Robin Hood public house. The crowded but lively settlement grew up above High Hill ferry from the eighteenth century. Although there were large local employers – a laundry by the railway viaduct and a chemical works to the north – many made a living from the boating and associated visitors. There was always a risk of flooding to the houses near the Lea and bad floods in 1928 and 1930 prompted designation for clearance. The tiny houses were replaced by the London County Council estate in 1937–8.

31

Caroline Cottages, which lay on either side of Caroline Street (the present Charnwood Street) and date from the 1820s, are seen here in 1912. These houses would probably have been home to men working on the adjacent plant nursery and brickworks in the nineteenth century and were to be cleared in 1927. Charnwood House, dating from 1937, now occupies the site.

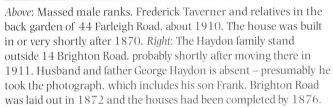

Above: Massed male ranks. Frederick Taverner and relatives in the back garden of 44 Farleigh Road, about 1910. The house was built in or very shortly after 1870. *Right*: The Haydon family stand outside 14 Brighton Road, probably shortly after moving there in 1911. Husband and father George Haydon is absent – presumably he took the photograph, which includes his son Frank. Brighton Road was laid out in 1872 and the houses had been completed by 1876.

No. 183 Lower Clapton Road was part of a row dating from the early eighteenth century. In about 1910 William Gaviller, whose family had owned the house for the previous hundred years, commissioned a set of photographs of the ground-floor rooms of the house and the garden. In this view the large bay room alongside the main house on the left is just visible.

A corner of the study. The series is a useful source for interiors of local upper-middle-class houses of the period. One of the paintings in the corner looks to be of Castle Hedingham in Essex. William Gaviller died in November 1913, after which the house passed into the hands of the Salvation Army. It was badly damaged by fire in December 1927 and the shell was demolished in March 1933 for the construction of the Powell House estate.

Possibly the dining room looking across towards one of the curved bay windows. Much of the furniture in the house shows the influence of William Morris. The painting above the door on the right looks to be of another Essex subject, the old church at Chingford, much painted by artists in the late Victorian era. The Gavillers also commissioned autochrome views of their greenhouse and garden, and these coloured glass plates are the earliest colour photographic views of any Hackney subject.

Newspapers were no longer the only source of news by 1914. This is the Hackney Picture Palace, one of the new cinemas on the west side of Mare Street. The adjoining property, the former Electric Picture Palace, closed prior to the demolition of the building to widen Graham Road. The summer boaters of the men and absence of coats suggest that this was taken in the early months of the First World War.

Another of Hackney's lost cinemas was the South Cinema at 133–7 Well Street, photographed in 1915 from the junction with Cassland Road. It had opened as the South Hackney Picture Palace in 1913 and lasted until about 1944. The building survived the war and was not demolished until the mid-1960s.

A social gathering of *quite* another kind. This is an afternoon tea party in the garden of the vicarage of St Thomas Church, Stamford Hill, about 1910. Best hats and frocks are to the fore, one guest on the left has half turned to the camera to share a conspiratorial thought . . . in another place this could have been an Impressionist painting. . . .

BOROUGH OF HACKNEY.

AIR RAID WARNING BY SYREN.

Notice is hereby given that the Syren which has been fixed at the Electricity Works, Millfields Road, to give Air Raid Warning will be sounded at **1 p.m.** on **Monday and Tuesday next,** the 18th and 19th February, 1918, and possibly **Wednesday,** the 20th February, 1918, for Testing Purposes only.

The public are requested to entirely ignore the signal on the above-mentioned hour and days.

14th February, 1918.

Norman George
Acting Town Clerk.

TOWN HALL,
MARE STREET, E.8.

The First World War was fought on the home front as well as in the trenches of France and Flanders. The first Zeppelin air raid over England passed across Hackney and Stoke Newington in May 1915, and the first bomb fell behind the Nevill Arms in Nevill Road. The 'syren' song was no longer a classical reference but a reality that warned of death from the air. Hackney and Stoke Newington were also much exercised by volunteer fund-raising and flag days. Another of Hackney's poster campaigns urged its citizens to raise support for a local benefit concert to 'Fight the Submarine in Your Homes', an injunction that conjures up an image of periscopes rising up through the drainage system, but at the time represented the threat to food supplies constituted by the German U-boats.

A 'Tank' day in Stoke Newington Church Street on 16 March 1918. There was hardly a day when Stoke Newington's streets were not cluttered by one flag-selling faction or another, but the introduction of the tank had had a powerful propaganda effect on the home front, billed as a secret weapon that would win the war. Mayor Herbert Ormond is one of the three figures on the tank's top doing his bit to raise custom for war bonds. The 'tank bank', a lottery and a brass band blasting out 'Hearts of Oak' raised over £112,000 in war bond purchases.

Digging for victory in Clissold Park on 24 March 1917, when the first sod was cut for wartime allotments. Not everyone was so patriotic. The Brotherhood Church in Southgate Road was the site of several pacifist meetings, one of which, on 28 July 1917, was attacked by supporters of the war and a riot ensued.

The war ended in an armistice on 11 November 1918. This local peace party was held in Digby Road in 1919.

Roaring Twenties?

Stoke Newington's war memorial took the form of a hall added alongside the library, which included a wall plaque with the names of those who died on active service. This view shows the dedication service in June 1923. Guests included Field Marshal Sir William Robertson. Despite the best efforts of a committee, there were some small mistakes and the odd omission, but the plaque constitutes the most comprehensive record of war dead erected by the three boroughs that today make up the London Borough of Hackney.

The Grange, one of the houses in Paradise Row, the western end of Stoke Newington Church Street, was up for sale in 1929. For over forty years it had been the residence of Frederick William Turner (1833–1928), the chairman and managing director of investment and mining companies. Advertised as suitable for redevelopment, the Grange was demolished about 1930 and replaced by the present Grange House and industrial buildings on the site of the garden.

This is 3–4 Glebe Place, also part of Paradise Row, in 1928. Four houses were built by Thomas Widdows about 1835. A recent customer at Hackney Archives Department identified herself as the then very new baby resting in the pram by the front steps. The Glebe Place houses were demolished about 1935 by the London County Council and Gaskin House now stands on the site.

In transition. This is Stoke Newington High Street, about 1925, looking north towards the Tyssen Street junction. Hackney Borough Council's distinctive electric street lights can be seen in the middle distance, but the only light traffic is all horse powered. Much of the late nineteenth-century rebuilding is in evidence, but the two-storey butcher's shop on the far left is a reminder of the appearance of much of the road only forty or so years before.

Still no traffic, but in anticipation there is a policeman on point duty at Newington Green in 1925. Regular traffic direction duty became a common part of police work before traffic lights became so widespread. The branch of Barclays Bank was built in 1892 after road widening. Newington Green Unitarian Chapel dates from 1708 and was refronted in 1860.

Left: The view west along Stoke Newington Church Street from the junction with Albion Road. The old Rose and Crown is on the left and the second house on the right of the junction is the eastern wing of Halstead House. This had been built with a central bay and two wings, each only one room thick that projected forward to street level, and although the construction date is not known, was built before 1741. It had been divided into three properties by 1848 and was to become a casualty of road alterations in 1930. Pencil sketch of 1926. *Right*: Austin Buildings, sketched by antiquarian Florence Bagust in 1929, was one of the small courts on the west side of Lower Clapton Road, south of St James Church. The atmosphere that impressed the artist eluded Hackney Borough Council which earmarked the narrow yards for slum clearance. The Ritz Cinema was built on the site, opening in 1939 and closing in 1973. The cinema had been demolished by 1980.

Egerton Road was formed out of the Craven Park estate, one of the last of Hackney's former large estates to be built over. Development was under way in the late 1890s. The New Synagogue in the centre of this view, *c.* 1925, was opened on 21 March 1915, when guests included Stoke Newington's Mayor Sir Herbert Ormond and Sir Marcus Samuel, the first Jewish Mayor of the City of London. The congregation had moved from a synagogue in Great St Helens, built in 1838.

Dalston Lane looking west towards Dalston Junction, about 1920. On the left is the Dalston Theatre, which had opened in 1886, housing a circus until 1890. This building was completed in 1898, but became 'Europe's first super cinema' in 1920. As the Dalston Gaumont it closed in 1960 and latterly has been the Four Aces, an Afro-Caribbean club. It is scheduled for demolition in 1999 as part of the redevelopment of this part of Dalston Lane. On the other side of the road the Dalston Picture Palace had opened in 1910 at No. 17. Closed by 1917, Nos 17–19 were later used as a billiard hall and then by Reeves, the artists' suppliers.

A view at the edge of Hackney, looking east along Hackney Road, with the Queen Elizabeth Hospital for children on the left, about 1925. The hospital lay just inside Bethnal Green, but served Tower Hamlets and Hackney until closure in 1999.

Looking north along Curtain Road from the Great Eastern Street junction, about 1920, the photographer has picked a quiet time. The barrows resting on the right are for the transport of furniture, for Curtain Road had become a centre for the wholesale traders from the 1860s onwards. They replaced the late eighteenth-century houses with modern warehouses, some equipped with showrooms. The 1920s saw the introduction of plywood and a gradual move of furniture manufacturing out to the Lea Valley.

The junction of Old Street and Kingsland Road, seen from the top end of Shoreditch High Street, about 1920. Electric trams cross at the western end of Hackney Road, but otherwise horse traffic predominates. In the centre is the original North London Railway station of 1865, demolished in 1927. The replacement, repaired after war damage, still survives as business premises.

The corner of Shoreditch High Street and Commercial Street in 1924 was dominated by the bulk of Bishopsgate goods station. This had been the site for the Eastern Counties Railway terminus in 1840, but after Liverpool Street station was opened, the station was rebuilt as a goods depot with work completed in 1881. A fire in 1964 did considerable damage and much of the upper levels were afterwards demolished. In use as a car park for many years, an ambitious scheme is in hand to convert the space for residential use.

'Loch Fyne haddock, *6d* a pound.'
Mr Portway's fish stall on Chatsworth
market in 1928.

Mare Street and Well Street were the
focus of the Hackney shoe trade by the
1920s. Here women are working in the
tipping shop at Frank & Co.'s factory in
Silesia Buildings, Mare Street, about
1920. The trade in Hackney dated back
to the 1880s, originally concentrated
round the south-east part of London
Fields. By the 1930s Hackney firms,
many of them having begun as Jewish
family businesses, dominated the North
London trade.

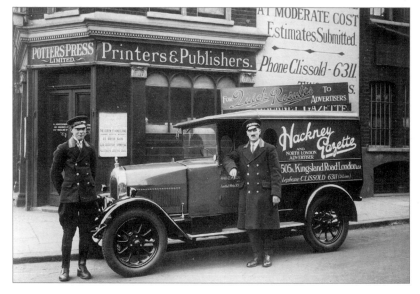

Motor transport comes to the *Hackney
Gazette*, as a van driver and his mate pose
outside the Kingsland Road offices. It is
March 1922 and Queen Mary has just
visited Shoreditch, so there will be lots to
read about.

The shooting of *Chu Chin Chow*, starring George Robey, is in progress at the Gainsborough Film Studios on Poole Street in 1934. American Paramount bought a former power station in 1924 and the studio was used by three successive British companies, one of whom created the Gainsborough Lady, which it used as its logo. Alfred Hitchcock filmed here and stars included Margaret Lockwood. Since closure in 1949 the building has seen a variety of business uses. Threatened with demolition several times over the last ten years, there is now a new proposal to reopen it as a film studio.

A more typical Shoreditch business scene was recorded in Dorset Mews, off the east side of East Road, about 1920. This yard adjoined the undertaking business of Dotteridge, founded in the late eighteenth century and which was based here and in the adjacent former Conservative Club on 27 New North Road until 1985.

Batey's Britannia Steam Works were at 216 Kingsland Road, in the section between the canal and Laburnum Street. William Batey established a ginger beer factory on the site in 1853 and the business survived until it was sold to Charrington & Co. in 1952.

Left: No. 4 Kingsland Road was in use as the local hostel of the Young Men's Christian Association in 1920. It had been built as the second building of the Shoreditch Charity School in 1799. When the school closed in 1889 the statues of a woman and two children were removed from the central niche, which was converted to a window. In recent years the premises have been used as a betting shop. *Right*: The Olympia Cinema at 203–4 Shoreditch High Street, not long after it had been converted from a theatre in 1926. It had begun as the Standard Theatre in a small converted shop in 1835, being rebuilt after a second fire in 1867 and again in 1897. There were plans to rebuild it into a far grander cinema and demolition cleared the site in 1939, but the war intervened and the site was left empty into the late 1950s.

A pub with presence – the Unicorn, 32 Shoreditch High Street, looking south-east along Commercial Street in the 1920s. Electric light fittings adorn the outside of the building and it has been covered with adverts for the brewery, but otherwise is little altered from how it had appeared in the 1870s. T.E. Cross & Sons also owned the Pembury Tavern on Amhurst Road.

After the end of the First World War, local unemployment increased. In September 1921 there was a rally of over 1,000 of the jobless outside Hoxton Church and the men marched from there to Kingsland Road to demand either employment or adequate maintenance payments from the Shoreditch Board of Guardians, who were in session. A deputation was received by the guardians, but no promises were given. After listening to several fiery speeches on the steps, the crowd dispersed.

A photograph opportunity presents itself for the Shoreditch Liberal candidate, Harold Reckitt, during the general election campaign of May 1929. The firewood seller and the small crowd are in Essex Street (now Shenfield Street). Reckitt's opponents were Viscount Knebworth (Conservative) and Ernest Thurtle, the sitting MP. Thurtle was re-elected, polling 20,552, giving him a clear majority of 7,571 over Reckitt.

A country dancing display at Tottenham Road School in 1923.

The high jump at Dalston County High School's sports day on 11 July 1928. The school was still at its original site in Colvestone Crescent and the games were held on the school field. Events included a sack race, a slow bicycle race and special event for the mistresses, a tin-balancing race. When Lady Holles School moved from its Mare Street buildings (now part of Cordwainer's College) in 1934, the High School took them over for junior pupils, which eased the pressure on the Colvestone Crescent buildings.

A group of children on the steps of Enfield Buildings, Aske Street in 1925. Enfield Buildings were erected by the Metropolitan Association for Improving the Dwellings of the Industrious Classes in the early 1880s and survive today, renamed Enfield Cloisters.

A charabanc and a dozen buses have assembled in Ivydale Road in the 1920s at the outset of a special away-day, as crowds and a clown look on. Neither the date or the occasion are known. Any ideas?

A dustman's holiday this time, as the crew of No. 7 cart from Shoreditch are all ready for a day out, possibly to Epping Forest. Earnings at the time were around £2 per week, with 3d extra for snow clearing.

Laying the foundation stone for St Augustine's parish hall in Yorkton Street, Shoreditch on 26 December 1926. The figure in glasses on the centre left is the colourful (and High Church) incumbent Father H.A. Wilson, whose portraits of life in an inner London parish during the Second World War included the splendidly titled *Death over Haggerston*. The parish hall was to be a vital part of the social as well as the religious life of this active church in one of the poorest districts of Shoreditch.

Love on the Dole:
the 1930s

By 1930 the population of Stoke Newington has just passed its peak
(52,172 in 1921). There was severe overcrowding in some areas, especially
in the south-east of the borough. Municipal housing was the answer, and
in some areas the larger middle-class houses were demolished for new
estates. The north side of Lordship Terrace gave way to a new estate, and
the Minister of Health, Hilton Young, and the Mayor, Alderman Gordon,
attended the opening of one of the blocks, Lordship House in 1934.

Church Street was altered considerably in the 1930s. Hanslip Fletcher sketched Church Row, Nos 166–72 Stoke Newington Church Street, in 1931, which dated from 1695 to 1699. Owned by the antiquarian Francis William Baxter, the four houses were bought by the council and demolished to provide a site for the new town hall, completed in 1937.

The top end of Albion Road was widened in 1933, work which involved the demolition of the nineteenth-century Rose and Crown building on the east side of the road. Halstead House went at the same time and the new Rose and Crown was built on the site. The top view shows the old pub, the bottom the new one with workmen putting the finishing touches to Kingsway, the parade of shops on the corner.

It was still easy for shoppers to cross
Kingsland High Street in the early 1930s,
even on what looks to have been a murky
winter's day. The photographer is looking
south, with the Railway Tavern on the right
of the view. The entrance to Ridley Road
market on the left and the domed building
just to the south was a branch of F.W.
Woolworth & Co., and is now the site of
Dalston Shopping Centre. J. Manger was a
salt merchant.

Shoreditch High Street had seen the growth
of great wholesale establishments like
Jeremiah Rotherham's millinery business
from the nineteenth century. This trend
gathered pace from the late 1920s. This
view shows the second-hand book stalls on
the west side of the road, just north of the
Bethnal Green Road junction. Brandon's
tailoring business survived until about
1929. The block was demolished in the
early 1930s and Lipton's bacon warehouse
built on the site in 1934.

Part of the west side of Hoxton Street,
about 1934, taken from the roof of Hoxton
Hall, looking south towards Crondall Street.
No. 165 is on the far right and the White
Horse public house (with the board
projecting from the first floor) is just visible
towards the rear. The view is prior to the
present refronting. An informal street
market started about 1850 and continues
today.

A bus is parked in Clifden Road alongside the Clapton Park Tavern and an ice-cream seller waits with his tricycle on the other side of Chatsworth Road, about 1935. The Clapton Park Tavern was built in 1869.

James Brooke & Sons' furnishing shop on the corner of Clarence Road and Mare Street is all decorated for the Coronation of 1937. This building had once housed another of Hackney's cinemas, the Hackney Electric Theatre, from 1912. This became the Clarence Cinema and closed about 1935.

There was a sizeable Jewish residential and business community in South Hackney, served by a number of shops in the Well Street area, including B. Smulevitch's bakery at 76 Well Street. Family and employees pose in front of what looks like a new shop front in the 1930s.

New goals for housing and public health were set in the early 1930s and Hackney and the London County Council began an ambitious programme of slum clearance. Photographic records were kept of what was to be demolished. This is the north side of Duncan Square, looking towards the backs of houses on the east side of the Broadway, about 1934. Many of the houses were in poor repair, suffering from damp and had been regarded by Hackney's Medical Officers of Health as slums since 1920. Duncan House (later Alden House) was built on the site by the LCC in 1935.

A wet day in Rosina Cottages, at the east end of Rosina Street, about 1933. The North London line lay behind the houses on the right. The houses were built by William Feast, a carpenter, who lived in Victoria Street (now Warneford Street), South Hackney, where he was responsible for houses of better quality than these. The area was cleared in 1938 and workshops now occupy the site.

A London fog hangs over Andrews Road and Antwerp Street in this view looking south across the Regent's Canal in the early 1930s. This area was designated for clearance by the London County Council in 1929, though demolition did not take place until after 1935. After the war the bulk of the site was used for factory units.

The Gothic windows of 6–8 Olinda Place suggest a building date in the late 1820s. These four-room cottages (and is the small brick building in the corner a shared outside privy?) stood on the east side of Stamford Hill south of the present Olinda Road and would originally have been agricultural labourers' cottages. All the houses in Olinda Place were cleared after 1936 and a builder's yard at the rear of Allison Court now occupies the site.

This was the combined living and sleeping room of 1a Big Hill in 1934, recorded as an example of what the public health service had to cope with as part of the rehousing programme. Prospective tenants could not simply bring their possessions out of their old homes and into new council houses. Fumigation of the better items was essential – and the rest would be burnt. In this case 'seventeen van loads of filthy and verminous furniture and effects were removed . . . for disinfection and destruction.'

These were the men who had to tackle the best that Big Hill could produce. Staff with their collection vehicles outside the disinfecting chamber at Millfields depot, 1934.

The interior of a Hoxton house, 18 June 1937. The photograph was taken to illustrate the work of the Hoxton Market Christian Mission, which provided boots, holidays, food and activities for local children. There were two adults and seven children living in this small house. The father, who was unemployed, was an atheist and the children had come on to the mission, so presumably a debate on the merits of religion is in progress. There is a gas cooker, the children are clean and well dressed for the time, but with only the eldest child at work, times would have been tough.

On the stump: Herbert Morrison canvasses South Hackney voters in 1935 for the Labour vote. Morrison had begun his career as councillor and mayor in Hackney in 1919 and began his parliamentary career as the MP for the constituency in 1922. Morrison lost the seat in 1924, returned in 1929 and lost it again in 1931. This time he was successful. Then as now election leaflets went through the door, but there was no substitute for direct communication with the voters.

Work was well under way on the construction of the Howard estate in the summer of 1938. The top view shows the walls of Hewling House and, in the background, Howard Road; the middle some of the workforce; and the lower, from alongside 64 Matthias Road, Hewling and Matthias houses almost complete.

There are few examples of 1930s architecture in Hackney, but in 1936 the German Hospital added a new wing, fronting onto Fassett Square to meet the need for additional beds for private patients. Designed by Burnet, Tait and Lorne, the new block opened on 10 July 1936. This a contemporary postcard showing the west front, with shared sun balconies designed for the benefit of patients.

In the days before the National Health Service, the Metropolitan Hospital relied on donations and private funding to provide for patients. Then as now fund-raising could be fun, and at the 1933 garden fête, held at 83–5 Lordship Road there were mayors aplenty to set an example. Stoke Newington's Mayor, Cllr Herbert Ormond, is on the left, accompanied by a colleague – while Cllr Bertie Bloomfield from Hackney looks on. Despite a chilly day there was a swimsuit show by models from Dudleys the drapers, fortune tellers and a comic dog show. The Metropolitan closed as a hospital in 1977 and the building now houses workshops.

The French Hospital on Victoria Park Road was an almshouse for people of French descent. This is the main gate and lodge in May 1936. The hospital moved to this site on the north side of Victoria Park Road in 1865, into a new building designed by R.L. Roumieu. After the hospital moved out in 1949, the premises were used by a convent school. Today it forms part of Cardinal Pole School. The lodge does not survive: the western part of the grounds, including the lodge, were purchased by the London County Council for construction of Banbury House in 1936–7.

Holland House, on the north-west corner of Newington Green, and dating from about 1680, had been bought by Edward Holland, who made ornamental chains. Holland converted some of the outbuildings into a factory. This view dates from about 1930, by which time A. Elmes' exhibition-fitting business had been in occupation for two years. Holland House survived the war but was demolished in 1965, with only the railings and front gateposts surviving. The factory buildings that succeeded it have in their turn been cleared for a housing and retail development, which will contain a short history and display on the lost Holland House.

What a lot of caps! The male part of the workforce of the Gas Meter Company of 238 Kingsland Road, just south of the Regents Canal, have assembled in the narrow works yard, about 1930. The photographer has his back to Kingsland Road. The factory was built on part of the site of the Independent Gas Company prior to 1883. Gas-meter making ceased in 1968.

The Hackney Furnishing Company claimed to have been founded by A.M. Stewart about 1870, though it is first listed in local directories in 1890. It also claimed to be one of the first firms to allow payment by instalments. By 1930 the firm offered insurance which would meet the payments if sickness prevented the customer from earning. The firm moved from the former premises of Green and Branscombe by the railway bridge in Mare Street to the town hall buildings, just south of the Reading Lane junction, where their extensive showrooms were stocked with antique, second-hand and new furnishings, and the favourable quotations in their brochure show that the press had been suitably flattered. This site will shortly form part of Hackney's New Technology and Learning Centre, incorporating Hackney's museum and main library, scheduled to open in 2001.

Electricity generation in Britain commonly began as a municipal initiative. This is Hackney's generating station at Millfields, seen from across the River Lea Navigation Cut in 1937. Constructed in 1901, and with later additions, the station was coal fired, with the fuel coming in by barge. Electricity was nationalised in 1947 and the bulk of the station was demolished in the early 1980s.

The Hackney and Stoke Newington Chamber of Commerce organised a trades fair at Clapton Baths, which was opened on 29 November 1933 by Prince George, who has paused at the mannequin fashion display. Among the fifty exhibitors were toy makers, furniture, drapery and the latest electrical goods. Radio Olympia displayed their Scandelli piano accordion, and local celebrity Phil Maurice and his Gipsy Orchestra used it to provide musical accompaniment for the fair.

The provision of public baths was as much about cleanliness as exercise, and cleanliness needed to extend to clothes. So baths also had municipal laundries attached. This is Gainsborough laundry in the 1930s. Standing on the west side of Gainsborough Road, the laundry was opened at the same time as the adjacent swimming baths, in October 1935. Facilities included six washing machines and washing, drying and ironing for a family of four cost 2s (10p).

Playtime for an infant class at Wordsworth Road School in the early 1930s. The school was opened by Hornsey School Board in 1878. The buildings were used as a school annexe from 1956 and were demolished in 1969. Horizon Special School now uses the site.

East Anglia, London and the eastern home counties all felt the effects of an earthquake on 7 June 1931. Traffic came to a halt as a water main burst in Great Eastern Street and in this view workmen are labouring to repair it. The majority of the damage was confined to falling roof tiles, though one unfortunate woman was hit on the head by a looking-glass.

The Savoy Cinema, 11–17 Stoke Newington Road, had just been completed when this 1936 photograph was taken and would soon be ready for its first presentation on 26 October. Seating 1,800, the cinema became part of the ABC group and closed in 1985.

The Hackney Empire on Mare Street, designed by Frank Matcham, opened in 1901. Seating 3,000, the theatre belonged to the Sir Oswald Stoll's theatre group. Stoll believed in family entertainment, and tried to exclude suggestive acts from his theatres, which led to a long-term ban on the appearance of music hall star Marie Lloyd. The Stoll group issued weekly programmes. The two variety covers are both from 1935; the majority of the productions were light musical ones, but there were also serious theatre pieces, like the 1936 details for the adaptation of Walter Greenwood's *Love on the Dole* in 1936. The Empire also served as an occasional cinema from 1910, and kept up Hackney spirits during the Second World War, but changing times brought about closure in 1956.

The year 1932/3 was a busy one for Shoreditch businessman and politician, J.E. Houseman. He was the founder and managing director of Bewells manufacturing chemists, at 19–21 Pitfield Street, and is seen in the top picture behind his counter. Houseman's speciality was 'Little Black Devils' cough sweets. As well as his business activities, Houseman found time to serve the community. He was a magistrate, a member of Shoreditch Council from 1917 and also served as a trustee of Cranston & Marshall's charity and as a governor of the City of London Lying-in Hospital. In common with many men in his position, he was also a Freemason. Houseman, a member of the People's Party and the local Liberal party, was chosen as Mayor in 1932/3, following Alderman W.J. Fudge. He determined to make his mayoral year a very active one. His exploits included driving an Underground train, firing a London & North Eastern Railway B12 express engine out of Liverpool Street to Ipswich on 3 October 1933 (bottom left) and visiting the submarine *Sturgeon* at Chatham on 26 October 1933. Houseman and his wife have just emerged from below deck with their guide, Lieutenant Roberts (bottom right).

War and Austerity:
the 1940s

Queen Elizabeth (the present Queen Mother) inspects members of Stoke Newington's Air-Raid Precautions staff on 23 May 1940. The Queen visited the Clissold depot, escorted by Admiral Sir Edward Evans, and also met nurses and stretcher parties.

A warden's post at Lebon's Corner, Dalston Lane, in May 1939. The Home Office had issued circulars about civil defence as early as July 1935. Shoreditch, with its pacifist Labour MP Ernest Thurtle and deputy Mayor, his wife Dorothy, daughter of George Lansbury, rejected the idea of air-raid precautions. Stoke Newington complied, though there were local protests. Hackney in contrast became the first local authority in the country to produce a local defence scheme.

Inside the Lebon's Corner post, May 1939. Recruitment of voluntary wardens started in Stoke Newington in March 1938. By September of that year Hackney's wardens had all but completed a borough-wide house-to-house visit to fit all residents for gas masks. This was accompanied by vigorous trench-digging activities on Hackney's various open spaces, but though enough earth was shifted to hold half the local population, no one could quite decide what the trenches were to be used for. What was really needed were deep shelters, and these the government was not prepared to construct for civilian populations because of the cost.

Food rationing was introduced in January 1940. U-boat attacks on convoys had reduced the flow of vital supplies of imported food. Some relief from the dominions did get through, and this distribution of canned food from Australia at Hackney Town Hall in 1942 was intended to help the poorer members of the community.

Hackney Council sent out photographers who compiled an extensive record of bomb damage, to add to the descriptions that survive in the 'incident' files. This first view shows the aftermath of an unexploded bomb that fell on the road in front of Nos 114–20 Mare Street, just north of the junction with Tudor Road on 7 September 1940.

Further up the road on the same evening, a bomb fell on the chemist's shop on Mare Street just north of St Thomas Square. These shops and a billiard hall on the opposite side of the road took the force of the blast.

Workmen pause in clearing the rubble from Mare Street and part of St Thomas Square on 8 September 1940.

Clearing up after a bomb that dropped in Cressett Street, also on 7 September 1940. The debate over the unfortunate chicken was in the back gardens of Collent Street, the site of which is now covered by Milborne and Collent houses.

Left: The effect of high explosives on 23–7 Glenarm Road on the night of 15 November 1940. The gap is now filled with 1950s housing. *Right*: Modern flats offered no more protection than Victorian houses to bombs. This block, which had replaced the houses on the west side of Lower Clapton Road just south of the Kenninghall Road junction, took a direct hit in 1940. The block was demolished after the war, and the site now forms part of the grounds of Gooch House.

Getting to work could be difficult in the aftermath of a raid – assuming your workplace had survived the night. This was Somerford Grove looking west towards Stoke Newington Road, with Simpson's factory on the left, on 21 September 1940. Simpson's factory is now the Turkish community centre.

Some raids could really be devastating. This is the Frampton Park Road junction with Darnley Road after a parachute mine fell on the night of 15 October 1940. The cameraman is looking north past the junction with the remains of houses on the north sides of Paragon Road visible in the middle distance, all of which were demolished after the incident.

After the spring of 1941, the amount of bombing raids decreased, but a new kind of menace affected Hackney from late 1944 onwards with the advent of the V1 flying bombs and the V2 rockets. One of the worst incidents occurred when the original Dalston Library, on the south side of Forest Road next to the junction with Woodland Street (later Forest Grove), was hit by a V2, which struck at 4.30 in the afternoon of 4 January 1945. The dead included two librarians, the wife of the vicar of St Philip's Church and two girls. The twisted metal frame in the foreground was the circular roof light of the library – virtually all that remained of the building.

Hackney Downs School pupils were evacuated to King's Lynn in 1939. However, many evacuee children returned to London, and some school buildings were reopened. Part of Hackney Downs School became an Emergency Elementary School and children attending the school are seen in this view that pre-dates July 1944. The 'road' and the crossing were marked out in the grounds of the school, and presumably the bus and car positioned to illustrate road safety conditions during wartime. The view is taken looking east with the school buildings on the right and parts of Birchington and Bicknor houses in the background.

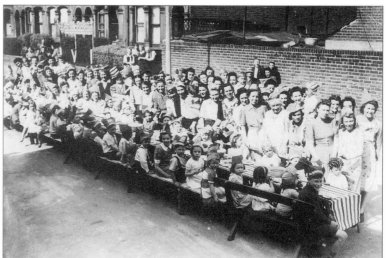

With victory in Europe came celebratory street parties. This one was in Daubeney Road on VE Day in 1945.

The aftermath of the war was an unfamiliar landscape, with open spaces where once there had been houses. This view was taken in January 1946 from Albion Road looking east. The southern part of Hawksley Road is on the left and Daniel Defoe Secondary School behind the trees. The end of Woodland Road is visible in the centre. Nothing remains of the former Cubitt houses on Albion Road or of the Sandbrook Road. Carlyle House now stands on the site in the foreground. Photograph, Sydney Newberry.

District nurses are about to begin the day's business in Shoreditch in the late 1940s. Shoreditch's Model Welfare Centre on Kingsland Road, behind them, and which opened in 1923, played an important part in local health provision, especially for women. With the creation of the National Health Service in July 1948, direct medical provision passed to the new health authorities, although local authorities continued to play their part in public health work.

Welfare services were the forerunner of today's social services. A woman worker from Shoreditch's domestic help section provides a meal to two local residents in 1949.

Domestic science was regarded as an important part of a girl's education. This is the cookery class at Dalston County Secondary School in 1947. Thirteen-year-old Gwendoline Larner posed for this view as part of a Ministry of Information portrait of a day in the life of one English schoolgirl, made for Australia.

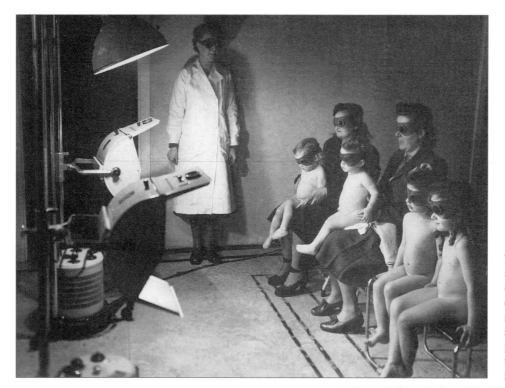

Tuberculosis was still a scourge in the 1940s. One of the treatments was exposure to artificial sunlight lamps and this somewhat surreal photograph was taken at the Richmond Road clinic in 1949.

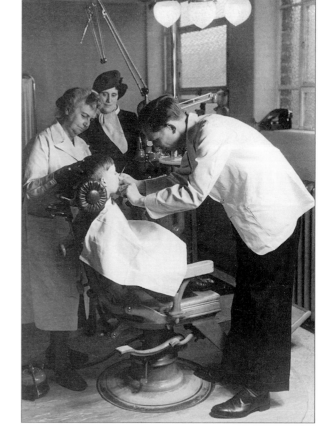

The National Health Service encompassed dentists as well as doctors, and one goal was the improvement of children's teeth. In the pre-war period it had been the done thing to have all your teeth removed and false sets substituted as a kind of preventative medicine; this was to change gradually in the ensuing decades. This child was being brave at the Richmond Road clinic, also in 1949.

The first stage of construction of a new housing estate. This was the Woodland Street corner with Richmond Road on 14 July 1948, with the last stages of demolition begun.

Progress has been made, with the five blocks on the east side of Forest Grove completed. Forest Road is in the foreground and Holly Street is on the left, 24 July 1948.

The formal opening of the Forest Road estate in Mayfield Close on 16 October 1948 by Hackney's Mayor, Cllr G.C. Carter. The ceremony was interrupted by heckling from residents of houses in Mayfield Road, scheduled for demolition. 'Fair play for the old people who are being turned out and put into dirty dives' was one cry and police had to be called in to protect the dignitaries.

Housebuilding could not keep pace with demand. One answer was the prefabricated house, which could be rapidly assembled on cleared bomb sites. These prefabs had recently been erected on Prince Edward Road (foreground) and Trowbridge Road. In the background is the roof line and chimney of Ingrams rubber factory. Although prefabs were supposed to be a short-term solution, some were to last for nearly thirty years.

Mechanical brooms and new dustcarts to keep Hackney clean. This was the line-up at Millfields depot on 21 July 1948.

Two of them this time! Just to prove that you are never very far from a rat in Inner London. A Hackney rat-catcher taking a pride in his work as part of a sewer-clearing operation, about 1949.

A church parade from St Mary of Eton takes the Annunciation to the masses, as it passes along Wick Road in 1948.

George Ewer's Grey Green coach firm was offering excursions with its new fleet of Bedford Duplex coaches from its base at 55 Stamford Hill. The offices had once been a prosperous middle-class villa, built in the early years of the nineteenth century. The Ewer family business began as a carter's firm in Shoreditch in 1885. The first motor vehicles were bought in 1919 and carried goods during the week and people at weekends. The move to Stamford Hill was made in 1930 and new workshops built behind the house. The buses on the forecourt are all Bedford 'Obs' with Duplex bodies which Ewers acquired from 1946 onwards.

The works outing all ready for the off. Workers pose outside the Peerless Laundry, 10 Elsdale Street in the summer of 1947.

What about the brains in Hackney? The BBC broadcast an episode of *The Brains Trust* from the Methodist Central Hall in Mare Street, about 1948. In the chair was Kenneth Horne, later to become better known for his radio comedy shows, with a line-up that included regular panellists like Humphrey Lestocq and Claude Dampier, as well as locals, including Hackney's borough engineer, G.L.A. Downing.

Back to normal after the strains of the war years. Stoke Newington's Mayor, Cllr Sammy Fisher, reopens Stoke Newington's Clissold swimming baths on 7 April 1945 after a six-year closure. A gala was held the following week, presided over by the local MP David Wietzman, with challenge races and life-saving demonstrations.

The Pavilion Cinema at 290 Mare Street opened in a new building in 1914, designed by George Billings and seating over 1,600 in an auditorium whose decorations rivalled any Edwardian theatre. After the war the management supported a flourishing children's club and in 1948 the BBC filmed children making a club banner on the premises.

74

Young Elizabethans:
the 1950s

'USE YOUR LIBRARY.' Taking books to the streets was Stoke Newington's contribution to the local celebrations for the Coronation of Queen Elizabeth II in June 1953, featuring Beryl Crago. The Queen visited the borough in the same year.

Brooke House, dating from the fifteenth century, was arguably the saddest loss to Hackney's builtheritage. It consisted of a Georgian frontage to Upper Clapton Road, behind which were two courtyards with many features dating from earlier centuries. In the 1530s it had been one of Henry VIII's residences and was known as 'The King's Place' before it acquired the later name from one of the owning families. Brooke House had been used as a lunatic asylum from 1760 to 1940, but it was badly bombed during the war. Both these views date from 1954. The top one shows the undamaged road frontage, the lower the devastation to the north quadrangle. The London County Council had acquired the site and, seeing no merit in restoration, proceeded to demolish the entire house for a new school. The only positive thing to come out of municipal destruction was a thorough building and archaeological survey as Hackney's only royal palace was lost forever.

The rise of television resulted in the beginning of the end for a whole type of Hackney buildings – the cinema. The Plaza at 538–40 Kingsland Road closed for good on 19 December 1959; appropriately the last bill included *Curse of the Undead*. It had begun life as the Kingsland Imperial in a converted shop. The altered premises are now a charity shop and a snooker centre.

Green Lanes, looking north to the Manor House public house. Trolleybuses were introduced in the 1930s and trams were gradually ousted from all routes. The electrically powered trolleybuses did not require rails to be laid – and maintained – in the roads, but did need a network of ugly overhead cables. This photograph was taken shortly before April 1952 when the last tram ran on route 33. Trolleybuses were introduced onto route 641 in May 1938 and lasted until November 1961. In an era of comparatively low car ownership both trams and trolleybuses had few traffic jams to negotiate and in today's terms represented environmentally acceptable forms of transport. . . .

. . . Or alternatively there was always the friendly tandem. The traffic lights at the junction of Brownswood Road and Green Lanes seem hardly necessary for the few vehicles on the road in this view of about 1952. The chimneys of the Pumping Station loom behind the trees.

Suburban Stoke Newington. This is Fairholt Road, one spring morning in the early 1950s with a United Dairies milk float doing the rounds. Many roads would have had iron railings, prior to the misguided scrap drive of the war years, but Fairholt Road, dating from the late 1880s, originally had wooden fencing, later replaced with brick walls and hedges. With car ownership comparatively uncommon, the photographer has captured the same spacious feel his predecessors achieved at the turn of the century.

Stoke Newington created a housing department in 1948 and then used its own direct labour force to rapidly increase the municipally owned housing stock. This photograph of 1958 shows the newly completed Rangoon House on the Burma Court estate, constructed to the north of Burma Road. The flats backed onto part of the course of the New River, which had been filled in south of the Park Lane bridge in 1946 and by 1958 was used as allotments.

Nos 1–4 Barn Street, photographed in 1955. These houses, which were built in 1869, were designated for compulsory purchase in November 1973 and the site used to extend St Mary Church of England Primary School.

Nothing like a pile of earth. Children at play on part of the newly constructed Woodberry Down estate, about 1950.

Construction of the Woodberry Down estate began in the mid-1930s. It was a London County Council scheme and aroused considerable protest from local middle-class residents, horrified by the prospect of East End urchins 'round my drinking water'. By 1950 the flats on the north side of Woodberry Grove were nearing completion. This view was taken from Eade Road, looking across the New River.

Two scenes from Woodberry Down estate of the early 1950s. *Left*: Two small girls go out to play. *Right*: Selling toffee apples.

Shoreditch Borough Council and the LCC also embarked on an extensive demolish and build programme. This was the junction of Cropley Street and Cavendish Street in 1953. The site was cleared by 1956 for the construction of Cropley Court.

The south side of Nichols Square looking west in 1953. Built in the 1840s, and long remaining a relatively prosperous enclave of Shoreditch, the council's decision to demolish it provoked considerable criticism, but it went ahead in 1963 anyway. Fellows Court now occupies the site.

The north side of Wimborne Street, looking west towards the junction with Cropley Street, early in 1951. The empty site on the right later became a playground, and the three rows of houses had all been cleared to build the Bracklyn Court blocks by the end of the year. The two-, three- and four-bedroom flats included built-in wardrobes and a fridge in each kitchen.

The Provost Street housing scheme had been Shoreditch's first exercise in municipal housing and also the first built by any London local authority other than the London County Council. Designed by Roland Plumbe, two blocks were completed in the narrow tongue of land bounded by Provost Street, Britannia Walk and Ebenezer Street in 1900. This 1951 view shows the courtyard side of Britannia Dwellings.

The sitting room of No. 11 Britannia Dwellings, 1951. In pre-television days the natural focus of the room is the fire place. a radio sits on the sideboard by the window and tea is about to be served. The flats were emptied by 1973 and the site cleared. After many years when the site was left empty, a new housing development is being constructed in 1999.

In contrast this is a Hackney bed-sitting room, about 1950, with bed, sink, gas cooker and table all in uncomfortable proximity.

Boating on the western of the two lakes in Clissold Park in the early 1950s. Attractions included a paddling pool, putting, bowls, tennis courts and even a miniature railway that ran through the trees and along the north side of the lakes.

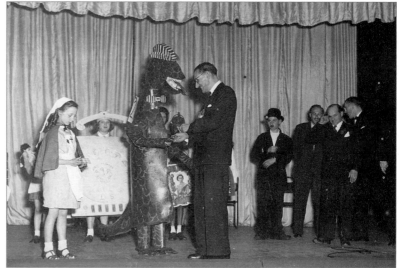

A close encounter during a children's show on road safety broadcast by the BBC from Hackney's assembly rooms in 1953.

And everyone can play with the cars and the trains, including the men from St John Ambulance Brigade. The elaborate model was also part of the same road safety campaign. There was considerable concern about road deaths and this model set up in Hackney Town Hall may have helped identify potential places of danger. Photograph, *c*. 1948.

The courtyard of the Geffrye Museum in 1949. The former Ironmongers Almshouses, dating from 1712, closed in 1910, when the almshouse moved to Mottingham, near Bromley in Kent. The buildings were sold to the Peabody Trust, who intended to demolish them. But by then the buildings were the last survivors of their kind in Shoreditch, and there was a campaign to save them from demolition and preserve the surrounding gardens. Eventually the London County Council stepped in (with some help from Shoreditch Borough Council) and bought the site in 1911. In 1912 the LCC agreed to convert the buildings to house a museum of furniture. The Geffrye Museum opened on 2 January 1914.

In the immediate postwar years, the Museum Curator was Molly Harrison, who wrote a wide range of historical source books for children on English domestic life. In 1950, when this photograph was taken, the museum had a room for children; after alterations this was used for refreshments.

How the library used to be. The children's library at the Homerton branch (now Chats Palace) in the early 1950s.

Inside F. Cooke's eel and pie shop, 41 Kingsland High Street, in 1955. The business was founded by Robert Cooke in Brick Lane in 1862. The High Street shop opened in 1910 and its marble and tiled interior, with the thematic mirrors, became a local landmark. Eels were kept in tanks at the back of the shop, and those destined for the table were transferred to a shelf at the front window.

Food inspection was part of the duties of the public health departments of local councils. A Hackney inspector comes face to face with a plaice at Mr Jones's shop at 6 Upper Clapton Road, about 1950.

Another Hackney inspector samples the milk at an unidentified grocery shop in 1951. In an era when the refrigerator was uncommon, canned goods made a greater contribution to home supplies.

Fancy dress parade at the Mandeville Street Coronation street party in June 1953. Among local attractions was a miniature display of the Coronation procession in the windows of Dudley's stores in Kingsland High Street. The model of the Queen wore a crown with real diamonds in it.

Hi de hi from the camp as the Butlin's choir prepares to do its bit for the Shoreditch carnival on 27 September 1958. 'Shoreditch to go gay', announced the *Hackney Gazette* in July. In advance of the carnival itself, Margaret Everton won the coveted title of Carnival Queen at a dance at the town hall. Her prizes included a free outfit 'and a super perm'. Margaret led the floats from an open-topped car on the big day and a week of activities followed, including the popular 'Yard of Ale' drinking competition at Wenlock Manor Hall.

Cllr Sammy Fisher copes with a point from the floor during the general election of 1951. David Weitzman was re-elected as the member for Stoke Newington and Hackney North, but after six years of power, Labour lost the election and the Conservatives began thirteen years of government.

Veterans march past the Crown at the top of Mare Street as part of the local commemoration of Armistice Day, 11 November 1952.

Princess Margaret was the guest of honour at the prize day at Hackney Hospital on 14 March 1957. Behind the Princess was Hackney's Mayor for that year, Cllr J. Kahn.

86

Swinging?
the 1960s

Emigration from the Caribbean to Hackney had begun in the late 1940s. Hackney Council's first body to address the issues of community relations was the Hackney Council for Coloured Citizens, formed in January 1959. This view was taken under the railway bridge on Mare Street, about 1962.

A Hackney panorama from the top of a block on the Trelawny estate across Morning Lane, about 1960. In the foreground, construction work on the estate is still in progress. Across the road are the prefabs put up on the bombed site of houses in Chalgrove Road, surrounding the surviving line of workshops (now the site of Tesco's supermarket and car park) while on the other side of the railway line the site south of Marks & Spencer is still vacant.

This was the view from Gooch House in August 1963. The cameraman was looking down on the site of today's Lea Bridge roundabout, with Lea Bridge Road running eastwards at the top of the picture. All the property on the north side back to the line of the garage in the middle top left of the picture was demolished for the roadworks. The scheme was completed by 1972.

Hackney continued to lose historic buildings in the 1960s. This was Spurstowe's Almshouses in 1966, on the verge of demolition. Founded in 1666 by a former vicar of Hackney, William Spurstowe, and completed on his land after his death by his brother, the six almshouses were intended for local widows. The small range, at the south end of Sylvester Path at the back of the Hackney Empire, had been rebuilt in 1819. They were replaced by new buildings on Navarino Road.

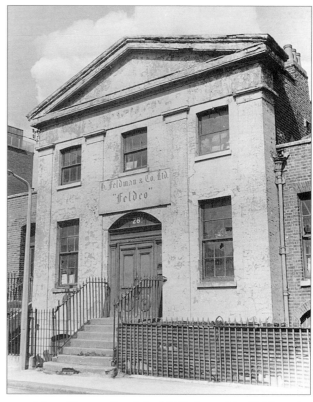

Left: The west front of the Salvation Army's Congress Hall, accessed from Linscott Road, in 1967. Opened in 1826 as the London Orphan Asylum, a charity founded by local philanthropist Andrew Reed, the asylum, which also served as a school, moved to Watford in 1871. The grounds were sold for development and the Salvation Army acquired the buildings in 1882, making them their headquarters until 1970, when a new citadel was built on Lower Clapton Road. All except the central portico was then demolished, and this surviving part is still the subject of debate as to its future use. *Right*: The central part of former Hackney Free and Parochial School building, 28 Chatham Place, in 1968. Completed in 1811, the buildings served the school until inspectors condemned the use of basement classrooms in 1893. Three years later the school moved again, this time to Isabella Road. The old school building survived in industrial use until it was demolished in 1973. Barbrook House stands on the site.

Homerton High Street narrowed considerably between Link Street and Isabella Road. This was how it appeared in 1960, shortly before roadworks commenced that widened the road and cleared the houses on both sides. The frontage of Marian Court now stands on the site of the houses on the right.

Left: The Crosby Head stood at the bottom of Pitfield Street on the Old Street junction by 1839. The memorial and drinking fountain are a link to the former Agnes le Clair spring and baths that stood on the north-east side of Tabernacle Square. This views was taken in 1964 shortly before the pub was demolished to widen the road. *Right*: The late 1960s were the era of 'flower power' and Hackney was not to be left out. No. 8 Glenarm Road is having the finishing touches put to its new image in 1967. Photograph, Frank Chambers.

Three faces of the working world in the 1960s begins with the inside of the furniture workshop of Saunders and Gable in 2a Appleby Street, the former parish hall of St Chad's Church. The modern and reproduction furniture trade remains well established in the Hackney Road area, but this business was displaced for the construction of Fellows Court in the early 1960s.

The offices of Smart Brothers men's outfitters on 117–19 Kingsland Road. Although taken in 1956 this scene was typical of many small businesses of the early and mid-1960s. The 'pigeon hole' unit on the left-hand wall would have been essential in a wholly paper-based era in which mechanical aids for the majority of businesses were limited to manual typewriters and possibly spirit duplicating machines.

The computer age had begun for larger employers in the 1960s. This is the new computer suite of Hackney Council on Southgate Road in 1967, with magnetic spools and tape printouts. Local authorities took advantage of the new technology to store their payroll and rating payment records; it is unfortunate for future generations of researchers that as the pace of technological change increased, records in old formats were not updated into new ones, so that much of the data generated by the machines in this picture has only survived in paper form, if at all.

Our 1960s trip out with shopping bag in hand starts at Harry Conway's reproduction furniture shop at 196 Shoreditch High Street in 1960. The shopfront is not quite as recorded in Thomas Tallis's series of drawings of the High Street frontages of 1838 and the rounded windows of the upper floors have been altered, but the shopfront was one of the few survivors of early nineteenth-century Shoreditch. Conway's business closed in 1980, but the building, which was listed Grade II in 1975, survives.

Inside H. & R. Englander's tobacconist's shop, 13 Pitfield Street in 1961, with pine counters and a mechanical till. Strip lighting provides a concession to modernity, but the shopkeeper has kept his enamel advertising signs. The small shop, just south of Charles Square, was cleared at the same time as the Crosby Head and Shoreditch House now stands on the site.

The interior of Tesco's supermarket, 405 Mare Street, about 1962. This was to be the shape of the grocery trade to come, although the range of goods was tiny compared to the stock in supermarkets at the end of the century. Tesco's, founded in Well Street market, later transferred the branch to the former Prince of Wales public house on Dalston Lane in 1967. This was demolished for the present housing estate in the early 1970s.

Ponies have been pressed into service to aid the protest against the introduction of parking meters in Chatsworth Road in May 1966. The Clapton Park Tavern is in the background. One meter scheme had been defeated, but in the long term the protest was to no avail. Photograph, Frank Chambers.

Serious stuff for the men on the Waste market on Kingsland Road in 1962. It looks as if the stallholder has got hold of some prize 78s and the second-hand books are being passed over.

Nests of coffee tables were no competition with Tubby's Sarsaparilla wine on the Waste market in 1969. The junction with Englefield Road is in the background.

A page of water starts with the Hackney Brook in 1966. The site of the railway bridge over Mare Street was once a ford, and courtesy of a burst sewer, the Hackney Brook briefly resumed its old course.

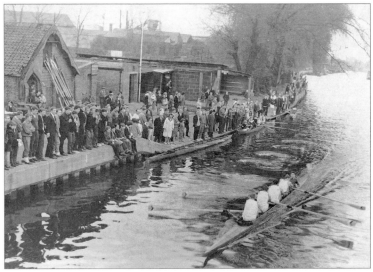

A cox and four pass Tyrells boathouse at Spring Hill during the annual Lea Regatta in 1965. Photograph, Frank Chambers.

Two barges are moored at timber yards on the section of the Hackney Cut that lies due east of the Kingsmead estate in 1966. The timber yards along the Lea provided the raw material for the Shoreditch furniture trade. This yard has been replaced by new housing. Photograph, Frank Chambers.

St Bartholomew's Church and vicarage, Dalston Lane, in 1968. Designed by J. Johnson and completed in 1884–5, the church closed during the Second World War. The parish was merged with St Mark, Dalston in 1953, but the church survived as a storehouse for church fittings from other redundant churches and was still in good condition when demolition began in 1968. The vicarage escaped the demolition men, became a listed building and a landmark of dereliction for over two decades. In the early 1990s it was finally incorporated into a new housing scheme. Photograph, Frank Chambers.

Left: Dedications to the Good Shepherd were sometimes used for mission churches, as was the case for this small Anglican chapel in Wilman Grove on London Fields West side, photographed in 1961. Built in 1889, the mission was served by clergy from St Philip's Church. After the destruction of the Church of St Michael and All Angels, London Fields by bombing, the congregation worshipped in the chapel until the new church was completed in 1961. It served as the church hall until 1970 and had been demolished by 1974. *Right*: Stamford Hill Congregational Church stands out in the snow, in this view taken from Dunsmure Road in 1962. The church, which seated 1,600, and an adjoining lecture hall, were opened in 1871 and had one of the largest congregations in Hackney at the turn of the century. But by the 1960s the building was too big for the congregation, who had the lecture hall adapted for worship. The church was demolished in 1966 and Stamford Hill Library completed on the site in 1968.

Hackney Downs School was founded on grammar school principles as a middle-class school for boys in North London by the Grocers Company and opened in 1876. It was run by the London County Council from 1907 and under the Education Act of 1944 became a county school, though still maintaining selection. The top view shows a science class in progress in 1962, and the middle one something of an interruption to a German class. 'Little Red Riding Hood is a small pretty girl and she – what did you say boy?'

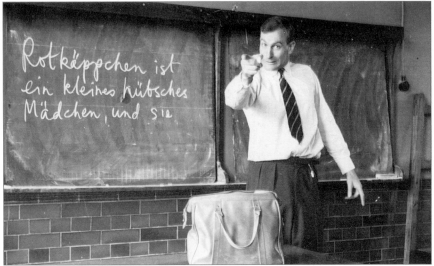

Radical change was to befall the school in the last three decades of the century. A fire that started in the school theatre after a dress rehearsal for a production of *Antigone* on 17 March 1963 gutted the main block of the school. So extensive was the blaze that the core of the original school had to be demolished. With the new buildings, opened in 1968, came a change to comprehensive status. A long period of problems in the late 1980s culminated in a government takeover by an education association, the first such action taken anywhere in Britain. The association closed the school in the autumn of 1995 and at the end of the century the site awaits a new use.

Making protest a social occasion. Pipers accompany tenants demonstrating about a rent rise for their Lakeside Court flats on Green Lanes, just north of what were then the filter beds, in the early 1960s.

From 1959 Holy Trinity Church in Dalston provided a home to the Clowns Gallery, a museum dedicated to clowns and their memorabilia. Clowns gathered annually for a service there, wearing full costume from 1967 and this view features the vicar of the time, Bill Sargent, with an array of talent who include (from left to right) Smokey (holding scissors), Harold Whiteley and Bill Sargent. The identity of the woman and the large-headed clown behind her are not known, but to their left are Tommy Keele, Alec Halls MBE (in top hat), Verdine (not certain) and Bimbo. The collection escaped damage in the Holy Trinity fire of 1985 and moved to its present location of 1 Hillman Street in 1994. Photograph, Frank Chambers.

A talent competition in progress in the gardens of Clapton Square in 1969. There was a proposal to construct a civic theatre here in the 1960s, but the money was not forthcoming.

A tricky moment for comedian and Hackney resident Monty Modlin at the fourth Hackney Annual Arts Festival in April 1969, as he looks around for inspiration on the appropriate one-liner. The festival developed from the Hackney art and drama festival which began in 1961.

Elizabeth Taylor lays the last brick that will complete the Pedro Club's new headquarters in July 1969. Miss Taylor had been asked to serve as vice president of the club by Sheran, Lady Hornby, chairman of the club and a childhood friend of the film star. Hundreds of people crowded into the street to see Miss Taylor arrive in a white Rolls-Royce. When told that the new clubhouse included a carpentry workshop big enough to build a thirty-foot boat she said 'You should have aimed at something a lot bigger, then you could have been able to build Richard [Burton] and me another yacht!' Founded in 1929, the club celebrated its 70th anniversary in 1999.

Local hero. On 18 October 1967 John A. Walter, originally from Nigeria, saved the two children in the photograph from a fire in a neighbouring house in Brighton Road. He received a certificate from the Society for the Protection of Life from Fire in February 1968, when this photograph by Val Wilmer was taken.

Protest and Jubilee: the 1970s

When it was discovered that the North London Line formed part of the route used to transport nuclear waste, there was strong local protest. Hackney was home to some of those active in the Campaign for Nuclear Disarmament, but this was an issue that awoke fear in those residents whose houses backed onto the railway. The assurances by British Nuclear Fuels that the casks would remain unbroken in the event of a railway accident were not believed. This march, organised by the Hackney Anti-Nuclear Group, took place on Kingsland High Street in July 1979.

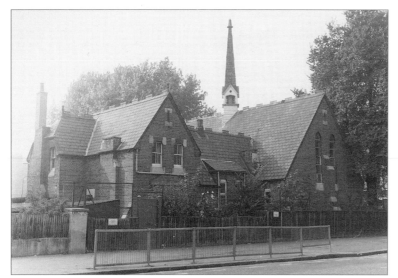

Rams Infants School stood on the corner of Tresham Avenue and Urswick Road and was recorded here shortly before demolition in 1972. The school had been one of Rams Episcopal Chapel Schools, opening in 1871 to accommodate 140 infants. The schools became part of Hackney Free and Parochial Schools in 1953; the modern successor infant school is at the west end of Mehetabel Road. Photograph, Arthur Wright.

Houses at the west end of Well Street near the junction with Mare Street, seen in 1970 shortly before demolition. The four-storey terrace whose end is just visible on the left was part of Denmark Place, built by local resident Hylton Dennis Hacon (whose ancestors were Danish) between 1802 and 1821. The ABC Cinema on the corner was built as the Regal and opened in March 1936; it ceased to be a cinema in 1981. After a variety of uses including snooker, it was in the course of demolition in June 1999.

Dawson's Corner in the narrow site between City and East Roads had been a landmark from the turn of the century. The shop had once been a drapery, but had expanded its ranges before closing in 1972. This view was taken in 1979, shortly before John Webb's furniture business closed and the whole block was demolished.

The view from a window in Hackney Town Hall in 1970. By this stage the Hackney Empire was a Mecca bingo hall. The Hackney Pavilion had another two years before closing on 22 January 1972 with *Carry On At Your Convenience*, hopefully not an injunction to former customers. It was then demolished and the site left vacant until the construction of the present branch of Barclays Bank and council offices in the 1980s. The empty site alongside the cinema was used briefly by the Air Training Corps, who put up a wooden hut there, but otherwise remained unbuilt on from 1908. It is proposed to build a new public house on the site in 2000.

Another of Hackney's vanished cinemas was the Essoldo on Mare Street, just south of St Thomas Square. Crowds queue for a bingo session in the early 1970s. The first cinema on the site was the Empress, converted from the former St Thomas Square Chapel in 1912. It was given a new front in the early 1930s and closed as a cinema in 1967. Bingo ended in 1995 and in the following year construction was under way for a new residential block for Cordwainers' College.

Hackney Wick has seen three successive transformations in the last 130 years. This was the west side of Chapman Road, looking north to the junction with Wick Road, in 1970. Built in the mid-1860s as part of what was originally named Elgin Street, this row survived the first phase of the construction of the Trowbridge estate in the late 1960s – the tower block in the centre is Hannington Point. This area was further transformed by road alterations following on the construction of the East Cross route from 1971 onwards and the altered course of Chapman Road now runs through the site. Hannington Point was one of Hackney's tower blocks to be blown up and the site was incorporated into the new Wick village.

By the time it was abolished on 31 March 1965, Shoreditch Borough Council had completed a radical transformation of its housing stock, replacing much of the nineteenth-century terraces with council estates in a little over a decade and a half. Taken in the 1970s from the roof of the Fellows Court estate community centre, this view looks east along Kent Street to the junction with Thurtle Road. Godwin House is in the foreground. The open space in the centre of Queensbridge Court marks the site of St Mary's Church, Haggerston, bombed in 1940. Beyond lies Haggerston Park, created from a combination of bomb sites and postwar house clearance.

Another building in the way of the East Cross route was the former Victoria Park station on Cadogan Terrace, seen here in 1970. This was the second station of 1866, which stood on the line down to Bow and the docks. Competition from buses affected passenger traffic, and the station was a victim of wartime economies, closing in 1942. Subsequently the whole of the line east of Dalston Junction closed for passengers. The revival of the mid-1980s restored a passenger service on the route to North Woolwich, but the Bow line closed entirely, though the course of the track remains. Photograph, Arthur Wright.

A view of the East Cross route under construction, as seen from Hannington Point in 1972. St Mary at Eton Church is directly below the camera and the rear of houses in Cadogan Terrace are in the background. The space to the left was the site of Victoria Park station.

Another view of the disruption caused by the construction of the East Cross route, about 1972. Hannington Point towers above the Victoria public house, on the corner of the stub end of Wick Road. Dwarfed between pub and tower block is the Eastway temporary library, housed in the wooden shed-like building. a replacement library opened in September 1979 but was closed in the cuts of the 1990s. The shops on the corner of Eastway have also gone, but the pub has survived all adversity.

Increased traffic on Hackney roads ensured that safety campaigns continued to be needed; this one for local children was held in 1975. Did the pedal car actually stop in time?

Balls Pond Road and Graham Road were badly affected by lorries en route to the docks or out to Essex. Members of the Balls Pond Road action group demonstrated in September 1979 after one man was badly injured and two women on Morning Lane narrowly missed being crushed by timber falling from a lorry. Eventually the GLC intervened with some controls over lorries crossing London and there was some decrease in heavy goods vehicles using the route.

British Rail renewed the bridge over Mare Street in 1973, causing considerable disruption to buses and cars. At this stage this part of the route was freight only.

Dalston Junction in the mid-1970s from the platforms. The redevelopment of Liverpool Street station spelled the end for the North London Line's City link. Services were retained while a new bridge and curve over Graham Road were put in to allow trains from Watford to be diverted into Liverpool Street, and then Dalston Junction and the line to the south closed in 1986. The track bed as far south as Worship Street survives, and is to be used for a new tube line in the twenty-first century.

Stoke Newington station, as seen from Hugh Gaitskell House in 1971. The Enfield branch of the Great Eastern Railway was completed in 1872. The present glass-box replacement building was completed in 1975. Photograph, Arthur Wright.

The barge and butty boat have just come through the sluice gates on the Hackney Cut near Weir Cottage, and this view was taken from Waterworks Lane in 1972. The building partially visible on the left is the disused pumping house built by the East London Waterworks Company.

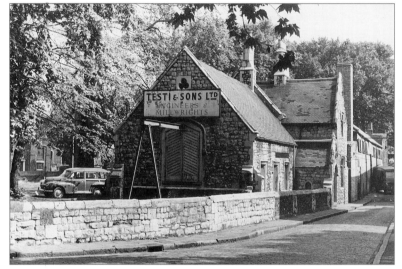

Testi & Sons' workshop on the opposite side of the lane once known as School Nook, alongside the Ship Aground public house, had been built as St James Infant School in the mid-1860s. It was later used as a mission church by St James Church, Lower Clapton Road, from 1888 to 1922 and from then on was utilised for a variety of businesses.

A pleasure boat has just passed beneath the Cat and Mutton bridge on the Regent's Canal heading for Acton Lock, on which the photographer is standing. Behind the bridge is the Walter Scott public house, which is now a Georgian and Russian restaurant. This view pre-dates the use by the Central Electricity Generating Board of the tow path as a route for high-voltage mains cables in the mid-1970s. Photograph, Arthur Wright, 1971.

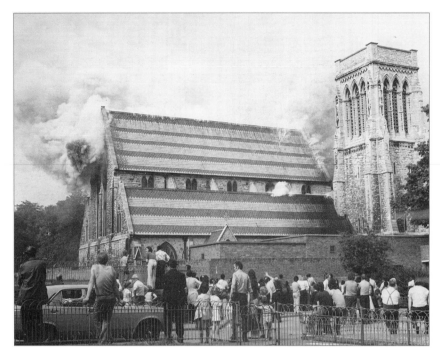

Fire broke out in St Matthews Church, Mount Pleasant Lane, on Sunday 6 June 1976. Worship on the site began in 1866 in an iron church, and the first minister was the assistant curate at St John at Hackney, L.E. Shelford, whom we have encountered in whiskered old age as prebendary of St Paul's Cathedral in 1900. The Kentish ragstone church was completed in 1867–9. Damaged in the Second World War, it was repaired in the early 1950s, but the 1976 fire proved to be the finale. The remains of the building were demolished in 1977 and replaced by the present brown-brick church. Photograph, Arthur Wright.

Left: The former Shrubland Road Congregational Church, on the south side of that road, photographed in 1972. Iron churches were supposed to be quick solutions to the problem of providing places of worship at low cost while congregations raised the funds for a conventional brick or stone building. This building, put up by Presbyterians on land that had belonged to the Rhodes family in 1858, became Congregational in 1871. One hundred years later the congregation merged with Trinity Congregational Church in Lauriston Road (itself now closed) and the church passed to the Evangelical and Reformed Church. It is now a listed building. *Right*: A memento of Shakespeare and Shoreditch. An actor presenting a model of the Theatre to the Mayor of Hackney, Cllr George Silver, in Shoreditch churchyard for the 400th anniversary of its building in 1976. The Theatre had been established by Richard Burbage in the grounds of the former Holywell Priory. It was taken down in 1598 and the materials spirited away to Bankside, where they were reused to build the Globe. Burbage's son Richard junior, another actor, was buried in St Leonard's churchyard and Shakespeare's plays were performed at another Shoreditch playhouse, the Curtain.

Queen Elizabeth II and Prince
Philip on the steps of the Queen
Elizabeth Hospital for Sick
Children on 6 July 1977, as part
of her Jubilee year visit to
Hackney.

Left: Patriotic fun from a clown at the Jubilee street party in Poole Road, 10 June 1977. Photograph, *Hackney Gazette*. *Right*:
'Never too old to boogie.' Ice creams all round for music men Alfred Tyler (then aged 70) on banjo, and Jack Hart (then aged
86) at the piano, helping with the Jubilee street party at Navarino Road, 10 June 1977. Photograph, *Hackney Gazette*.

A potato and spoon race for children in Lenthall Road, August 1978. The skips, scaffolding, piles of old doors and sheeted bricks are a sign of changing times, as houses that were formerly rented passed into owner-occupation. There was a stage in the late 1970s in some roads that successive cement patches marked the progress of renovation and rehabilitation for houses that would once have been earmarked for demolition.

Littlewoods linked up with Hackney Council to promote a local lottery in May 1978. Quiz show host Nicholas Parsons undertook its promotion and is creating a photo opportunity in Mr Patel's newsagent's shop in Kingsland Road. The lucky winner, who seemed uncertain as to what he was going to do with his winnings, received his prize at the Guildhall from the Lord Mayor.

All dressed up and somewhere to go. Turkish Cypriot girls in costume for the De Beauvoir Carnival in 1979. This became an annual event with floats and children's entertainments.

Labour was the majority party in the London Borough of Hackney from its inception on 1 April 1965. There was time for a little light relief in the council chamber in 1970. Long-serving councillor Alderman Bob Masters was renowned for his penchant for striking ties. Colleague Leslie House (left) has just presented Masters with a particularly vivid addition to the collection. The relaxed atmosphere was interrupted by a Conservative victory in 1971 on the back of mid-term blues for the then Labour government.

Another face of public services. This was Hackney Hospital, seen from Kenworthy Road in the 1970s. After the workhouse period ended in 1930, the former buildings passed to London County Council control as a hospital. The site was cramped and the monolithic workhouse blocks became increasingly ill-suited to modern medical standards of care. By 1976 prefabricated operating theatres were being installed, while one block earned the distinction of being 'arguably the worst general hospital psychiatric facility in the country'. It had to serve as an acute hospital during the construction of Homerton Hospital in 1985 and then as a geriatric and psychiatric hospital before demolition began – not before time – in 1993. Housing now occupies the site.

Hackney resident Peter Cooke drove his invalid car up to the Paris Theatre, Lower Regent Street, to meet disc jockey Jimmy Savile in October 1971 as part of Hackney Council's promotional efforts for the new Chronically Sick and Disabled Persons Act. The act empowered local authorities to count the number of people with disabilities in their area and record their needs. A motorcade of three-wheeled disabled cars did a round trip from Hackney Town Hall to Chatsworth, Ridley Road, Hoxton and Kingsland Waste markets to help get the message across to local people.

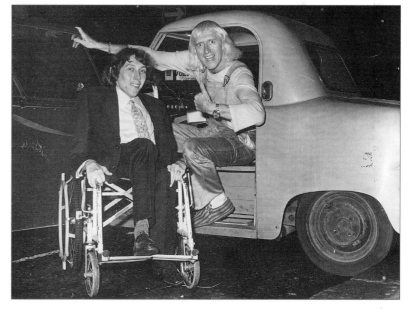

The 1970s saw the beginning of radical social changes to the role of women in society and to women's issues in general, including health. The Women's National Cancer Control Campaign mobile caravan was parked outside Hackney Town Hall in July 1971.

But a town hall dominated by men in senior positions, coupled with the advent of the miniskirt, had no problems in using female staff in promotional roles. This was a float for the launch of the Hackney Festival in 1972.

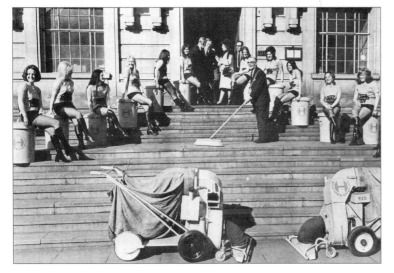

'Keeping the town tidy, or the day the Dustbin Dollies hit Hackney.' To publicise efforts to keep the streets clean, volunteer female staff dressed up in black hot pants, knee-length boots and orange tee shirts emblazoned with 'Keep Hackney Tidy' on the fronts. The publicity day, 27 March 1971, began on the steps of the town hall with the Mayor, Cllr Charles Hegarty JP and newly ordered street sweeping machines, and whatever else it achieved, certainly made the pages of the national press.

Michael Ferreira, aged 19, was knifed in Stoke Newington Road on 10 December 1978 by three white youths who were heard shouting National Front slogans. He was taken to Stoke Newington police station, but it was alleged that the police did not take action soon enough to call an ambulance. By the time Ferreira was transferred to hospital it was too late to save his life and he died two hours later. The reactions from the black community, including this meeting in Ridley Road, led to the formation of the Black People's Defence Organisation. This was to be just one of many cases concerning the alleged racist attitudes of Stoke Newington police. Photograph, Ernie Greenwood.

Music played an important part in publicising those opposed to the far right. The Rock Against Racism Concert was held in Victoria Park on 30 April 1978. This view from the stage catches the Clash in mid-number. Photograph, Val Wilmer.

The 1970s also saw the advent of punk. The Vomitones are seen here playing Centerprise for the Christmas benefit for the *Hackney People's Paper* in December 1977.

The law intervenes on Chatsworth Road during the dustmen's strike of 1970. This strike left Hackney streets piled high with unsavoury black bags, and the residue of market days uncleared. 'Its much sweeter inside', proclaimed one fashion shop window in the same road. Police were also called in to protect the external contractors who had to shift some of the worst of the rubbish piles, before the strike was settled. Photograph, Arthur Wright.

The miners' strike of 1974 saw pickets at power stations throughout the country, including Hackney's former municipal station at Millfields. Photograph, Arthur Wright.

Other unions also took to the streets in solidarity. This was part of a Hackney NALGO demonstration moving off down Mare Street in the same year. The miners were deemed to have won what they had gone on strike for. The next major national strike, in 1984–5, also saw considerable local support from Hackney, but ended in defeat and division.

Modern Times:
Hackney since 1980

Deputy Labour leader and transport spokesman John Prescott stands with Hackney Council leader John MaCafferty to support the long-standing campaign to bring the tube to Hackney in 1991. Although there are Underground stations at the edge of the borough, at Old Street, Manor House, and Shoreditch (physically in Tower Hamlets), Hackney remains the only London borough with no stations inside its administrative area. Promoted possibilities, including a Chelsea to Hackney route were mooted, but there never seemed to be funds available to get them started. At the end of the twentieth century, with Railtrack set to take on the maintenance of some London Underground tracks, there seems to be a promise that a new connection will be built from the Metropolitan Line's Shoreditch station to connect with the former North London Line City extension north of Worship Street to run to Highbury via Dalston Junction. However, the experienced Hackney tube watchers will not be holding their collective breath. . . .

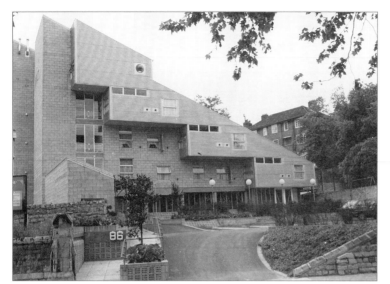

Housing issues have formed a steady theme through Hackney's twentieth century, but the issues became more serious with the perceived physical and social failures of the tower block estates of the late 1960s. Conservative policies saw the sale of council houses, even in Hackney, and regeneration and new building initiatives move from the council to housing associations. This is 86 Mount Pleasant Lane, twenty-one flats for elderly people built by Newlon Housing on part of the site of the old St Matthew's Church, which were praised by the Civic Trust in 1984.

The construction of the western end of King Edward's Road in the 1860s provided a splendid approach to St John of Jerusalem Church until the late 1960s, when the construction of the Kingshold estate, with its tower blocks, raised housing and aerial walkways and monolithic concrete car park block, broke up the street pattern. Part of King Edward's Road and the northern end of Handley Road vanished entirely and the truncated western end of King Edward's Road was renamed Moulins Road. The top view, looking west shows the result. Despite remedial action, which included the demolition of the car block and the aerial walkways (the latter having provided the perfect escape route for local thieves and muggers), the estate remained an eyesore and a concrete excrescence. Eventually grant aid permitted wholesale demolition and local residents took up the cry to restore the old street pattern. The lower view shows what had been achieved by 1998. Both photographs, Chris Dorley-Brown.

The industrial River Lea was also giving way to housing in the 1980s. This is part of the newly constructed Riverside Close estate, which replaced the huge timber wharves that once lay to the north of Mount Pleasant Hill, seen from a southward-heading excursion boat in 1987. Photograph, Author.

With hard-won government grants, Hackney was able to carry out improvements to some of its earlier estates, and show off its successes. The Lea View estate, begun in 1939, was redesigned and refurbished in 1985, with the participation of the tenants. The scheme included new sheltered accommodation for the elderly and solar heating panels. Prince Charles paid a three-hour visit to view the results on 1 April 1986.

Hackney was declared a nuclear-free zone in the 1980s. To emphasise political support for the revived anti-nuclear campaign, Hackney Council created a peace garden in St Thomas Square. Mayor Betty Shanks and Japanese guests, survivors from the Hiroshama bombing of 1945, pose at the opening of the garden on 7 August 1985.

The last moments of Highworth Point on the Trowbridge estate, 7 September 1986. The explosion was held up for an hour by a demonstration, but unlike the first such demolition, of Northaid Point in 1985, the tower block did not survive the blast. The end of the twentieth century will see the end of the majority of the tower blocks, built with such hopes and with considerable initial enthusiasm, before lift failures and vandalism changed tenants' minds. Photograph, Chris Dorley-Brown.

Green Machines? Chair of the Environmental Services Committee Cam Matheson (centre) leans on one of the newly commissioned street-sweeping vehicles in Mare Street's Narrow Way in November 1990. The state of Hackney's streets had been identified as an issue of considerable concern to residents, one of whom, Mike Butler, formed the Clean Up Hackney Campaign and is on the right of the photograph. Council worker Helen Rizzole and a Green Machine complete the line-up.

Left: Rectory Road refurbishment. In May 1985 the rebuilt station was opened by Hackney Mayor Ken Hanson, flanked by Dave Wetzel of the Greater London Council and Peter Sturt, British Rail's area manager based at Broxbourne. The booking hall and station buildings were rebuilt, a new stairway constructed and the brick work cleaned. The scheme was jointly funded by the GLC and the Department of the Environment. *Right*: The crew of a Titan bus on Route 30 pose obligingly inside Clapton bus garage in August 1987. With the division of London Transport's bus division into separate operating companies, combined with industrial action, many of Hackney's bus garages were under threat. In the event the modern Ash Grove garage was one of the casualties, and Clapton garage, off Mare Street, which originated as a tram depot for the North Metropolitan in 1871, survived. However, two other garages, Shrubland Road and Well Street, were axed as part of depot rationalisation. Photograph, Jenny Golden (Hackney Archives Department).

The success of Brent Cross shopping centre in the late 1970s spawned a host of local imitators. The Kingsland Centre (originally the Dalston Centre) opened in 1989 on the east side of Kingsland High Street. The supermarket at the heart of the original centre was one of the Co-operative's Leo chain, but it did not prove enough of a crowd puller. On closure, Sainsbury's moved their branch from the High Street to take its place and although some shops failed to survive, the Centre itself was well established by the end of the twentieth century. Dalston, with its large Afro-Caribbean community, was a popular place for the Nation of Islam to sell their newspaper, *The Final Call*, and in the late 1990s most Saturdays saw between five and twenty black-suited and red bow tie-wearing members on duty. Just such a group are discernable at the entrance to the shopping centre. Photograph, Author, 1999.

Left: The Dalston Peace Mural, on the west wall of 15 Dalston Lane. Designed by Ray Walker (1945–84) and painted by Mike Jones and Anne Walker, the mural was formally opened by the GLC's Tony Banks in October 1985 as another manifestation of Hackney's anti-nuclear credentials. Photograph, Author, 1999. *Right*: F. Cooke's eel and pie shop achieved immortality through the pages of *Eels, Pie and Mash*, the work of photographer Chris Clunn, who poses between Chris Cooke (left) and Fred Cooke (right). Sadly the owners decided that they could no longer continue, and in 1997 the shop closed its doors for good. The marble counters and mirrors decorated with eels were listed by English Heritage and have been retained by the Chinese restaurant that has taken over the Kingsland High Street shop. Photograph, Chris Wood.

The view from the stage at the Hackney Peace Fayre, held at the Town Hall Assembly Rooms in May 1981. The fayre was opened by George Melly, visible in the audience, just to the right of the central microphone stand.

The new leisure pool at the Britannia Centre brought a different kind of swimming pool experience to Hackney. The new pool was opened on 19 January 1985. Celebrity visitors have included Olympic swimmer Duncan Goodhew, seen with local children in the lower photograph.

Fashion with a difference at an event organised by the Hackney Pakistan's Women's Centre, *c.* 1985. The centre was based at 42 Stamford Hill; this event may have been at Stoke Newington's assembly rooms. The centre provided advice on social and cultural issues and classes taught in English and Urdu.

Canal adventure. Children canoe out from the Laburnum Boat Club inlet on the Regent's Canal, about 1986. In the 1970s the basin was full of rubbish. A jointly financed scheme by the Greater London Council and the London Borough of Hackney cleared the basin and funded the construction of the boathouse in the early 1980s. Today the club owns three narrowboats and runs sailing and canoeing programmes for children.

Men and women celebrate separately at a Hasidic wedding in Stamford Hill in 1983. Photograph, Mike Abrahams.

Afro-Caribbean record stall on Ridley Road market, 1982. Ridley Road market, which moved there from Kingsland High Street in the 1920s, has become multi-ethnic but remains a great place for fresh fruit and vegetables. Photograph, Val Wilmer.

Six sacked Turkish workers and the Trade Union representative picket the Queensland Pleaters garment factory in Elsdale Street on 9 October 1983. Attempts to have the management deal with fumes from badly ventilated rooms, poor toilets, a rodent problem and to raise the issue of wages resulted in an initial strike, a return to work and then further action, which brought about the sackings. The managing director recruited new staff and in the end the strikers gave up their action – one example of poor working conditions in some of Hackney's clothing factories.

Mentmore Industries provided employment for local people with disabilities in Mentmore Terrace, just east of London Fields, This view shows the inside of the factory in 1984. Although the area was zoned for light industry, the old Victorian houses, including the one housing the workshop, were earmarked for demolition by Hackney Council and a long battle ensued before eventually the Council gave way and the houses were saved. Photograph, David Hoffman.

The moment it all went wrong for one criminal.
An armed wages grab on a business in Seal
Street in 1990 was foiled when factory workers
grappled with the thief. Unarmed police then
prevented him from escaping. Photograph, Paul
Stewart.

Left: The death of Colin Roach in custody in Stoke Newington police station in 1983 led to considerable local protest and a campaign to seek justice. A demonstration near Ridley Road on 12 March 1983 led to police intervention, and the arrest of Colin Roach's father, James. *Right*: Hackney Council was also hell-bent on a collision of its own in March 1985. Tight controls on local government expenditure seemed to force council members, and in particular the Labour group, led by Cllr Hilda Kean, to make unacceptable cuts in services to local people. This was the scene inside the council chamber on 7 March, when the council failed to set a rate for the coming year. For two months the fate of the council hung in the balance, but at two meetings on 21 and 22 May the council increased the rate to the maximum allowed by the rate-capping legislation and set a legal budget. Hilda Kean and her deputy Andrew Puddephatt both resigned their positions, but not as councillors.

In 1986 Hackney Council invited Sinn Fein members to visit the borough and address councillors. Liberal Democrat member Pierre Royan disrupted the proceedings by firing a blank from a gun in the chamber. The top view shows the moment after the gun has been discharged; one of the Sinn Fein delegates is seated in front of Royan. The gun-toting councillor was restrained and ejected from the council chamber, and the address went ahead, applauded at the end by Labour members.

Council leader Andrew Puddephatt and Mayor Medlin Lewis launch the Hackney part of the People's Petition against the Poll Tax in the summer of 1988 in Mare Street. Comedian Harry Enfield – alias 'Hackney's best known kebab shop owner, Stavros' – has just signed in support. The Conservative Prime Minister Margaret Thatcher was determined to introduce the 'council tax', which was payable by all residents, despite advice to the contrary from inside and outside her party. For inner-city areas like Hackney it proved a nightmare to collect, and led to a drop in those registered to vote, as well as determined attempts by some to avoid being on the 1991 census in case that too was used as a means to enforce payment.

Diane Abbott makes her speech of thanks at Hackney Town Hall after the result of the May 1987 general election for Hackney North and Stoke Newington has been announced, making her Britain's first black woman MP. Photograph, Chris Dorley-Brown.

Hackney's two MPs, Ernie Roberts (left) and Brian Sedgemore, pose on the steps of No. 10 Downing Street with council leader Hilda Kean and the 'Save Hackney' petition, which also included support for the doomed GLC. The visit was part of a series of events that took place from October 1983. It was claimed that the campaign helped Hackney obtain more partnership money, but nothing could save the Greater London Council from abolition on 31 March 1986.

Tony Benn MP takes to the microphone on the steps of Hackney Town Hall in October 1983 at a demonstration to oppose the closure of the St Leonard's Hospital, Shoreditch, proposed as part of the focusing of hospital services on two remaining sites, St Bartholomew Hospital and the Homerton Hospital. In the event closure was implemented and the majority of the hospital buildings gradually demolished.

When American Cruise missiles were stationed at the Greenham Common base in the early 1980s, the issue of opposition became a critical one for many women. The Greenham 'wimmin' borrowed the campaigning slogan from lesbians to leaflet passers-by outside the Barclays Bank branch in Kingsland High Street on 29 March 1984. Photograph, David Hoffman.

Women also set up a peace camp outside Hackney Town Hall, which lasted from 29 February to 1 March 1984. The women put up 'benders', like the tents used on Greenham Common, played music and cooked supper over a camp fire each night. Although the campers attracted supporting comments from passers-by, the occupation was less than popular with some of the town hall staff. Photograph, David Hoffman.

The threat of AIDS brought about changes to how society faced up to issues of safe sex and contraception. This display was part of a women's health day at Brownswood Library in 1990. Photograph, Pam Isherwood.

The Hackney Empire reopened as a theatre in 1987. Mecca had removed the domes, and a long battle with the GLC Historic Buildings division was not finally resolved until Mecca had passed control to a newly formed trust, led by Roland Muldoon. In its new guise the Empire was one of the new comedy venues for many of those who went on to stardom. The bill for 4–6 June 1987 featured Julian Clary as Joan Collins' Fan Club, Harry Enfield, whose Stavros character was based on a local kebab shop owner, and Paul Merton. At the century's close, the Empire looks to have secured Heritage Lottery funding that will enable the trust to make vital improvements to Hackney's principal live theatre on the eve of its own centenary in 2001.

Index